Writing Myself Into Existence

Notes on a Literary Life and Other Adventures

An Abecedarium of Sorts

Arthur Asa Berger

NeoPoiesisPress.com

NeoPoiesis Press, LLC

2775 Harbor Ave SW, Suite D, Seattle, WA 98126-2138

Inquiries: Info@NeoPoiesisPress.com

Arthur Asa Berger – Writing Myself Into Existance
ISBN: 978-0-9903565-6-1 (pbk)

    1. Memoir. I. Berger, Arthur Asa II. Writing Myself Into Existence.

Library of Congress Control Number: 2015919379

First Edition

All illustrations and journal pages by Arthur Asa Berger

Design, art direction and typography: Milo Duffin and Stephen Roxborough

Printed in the United States of America

Dedication: Furor Scribendi

This book is dedicated to all the acquiring editors,
production editors, copy-editors, cover artists and
book designers, translators (my books have been
translated into nine language), manuscript reviewers,
and everyone else in the publishing world who have
helped me come into being as a writer.

Contents

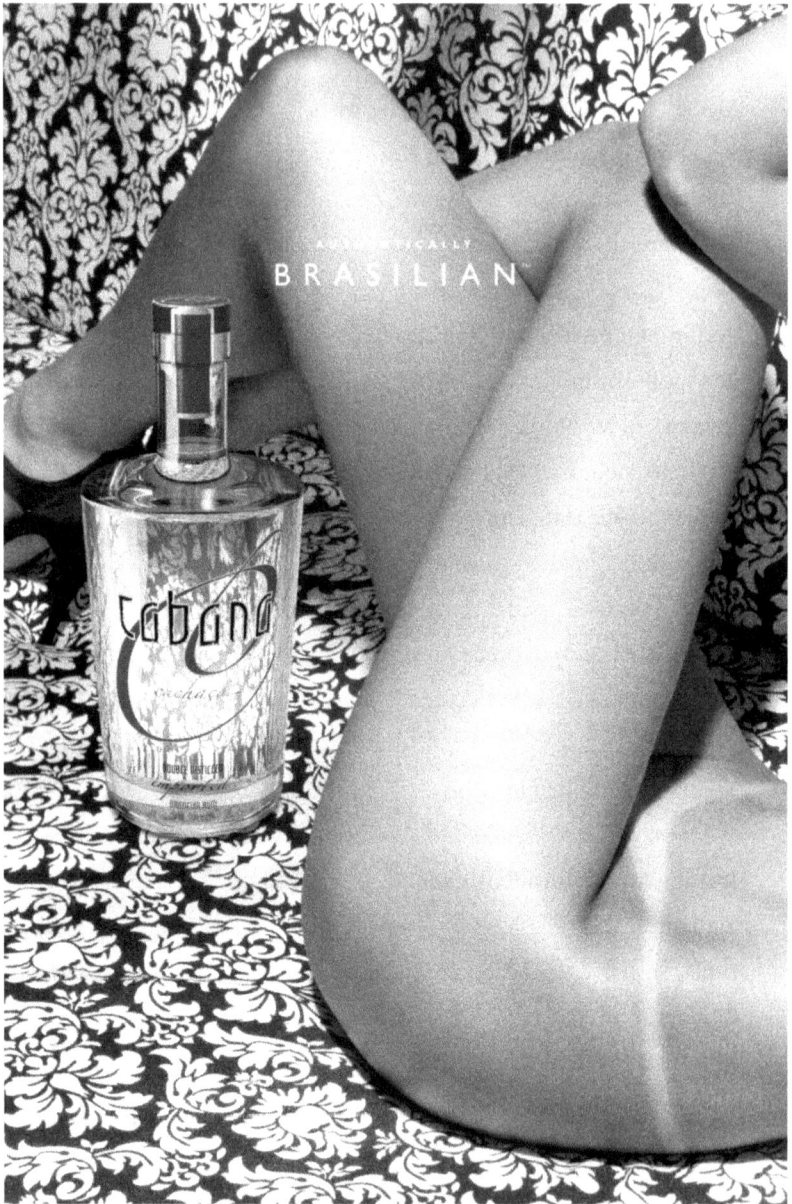

This advertisement for a Brazilian liquor is part of a campaign that has been attacked for exploiting the female body. Other ads in the campaign are similar in nature.

Advertising or The Agent in the Agency

I had an excellent Catholic education in high school, which is remarkable since I attended a public school and I'm Jewish. When I was in high school, at Roxbury Memorial High School for Boys (in Boston), I didn't have the slightest idea about what I wanted to do with myself. I knew that I liked to write and I liked to draw. What to do? I took many different tests—one of which was called the Kuder Preference Test, if I remember correctly—and they all came out with the same answer: go into advertising. Maybe it was because the tests recognized the creative aspects of my personality and thought that channeling this creativity into advertising made more sense than, say, becoming an accountant. Or maybe they discerned that I had a lot of potential as a flimflam artist?

I've always had negative feelings about advertising. I admire the creativity of many of the people in the business, but I am very uneasy (to put it mildly) about the power advertising has to shape individual behavior and the way it has created a consumer culture in which, as the saying goes, "in life, it's the boys with the most toys who win." In one of my books, *Pop Culture*, I wrote about what I called "The Affordinary Man" (and Woman), who measure life in terms of the goodies they can afford and measure other people the same way. For this so-called "Affordinary Man" (and Woman) the numbers on the stock market pages are of all-consuming interest (meant literally and figuratively) and determine how he or she feels about himself/herself and his or her place in the universe.

And it is advertising, of course, that helps shape the consciousness of these "Affordinaries," as marketers would put it. Marketers in the United States are always dividing the American public into different groups, based on things like age, sex, race, religion, zip code, socio-economic status, and consumption patterns. These groupings are supposed to help advertising agencies learn how to design their ads and commercials to appeal to specific groups that a company is targeting. We are constantly told that we are important as individuals ("We do it all for you") but for companies, what's most important is whether we're 18-45 years old and have a certain amount of discretionary income to spend—or that we're willing to borrow money to buy things we often don't need. And the advertising agencies are the ones who create the print ads and radio and television commercials that move so many of us in such profound ways.

Some television commercials are absolutely brilliant works of art, or of persuasive art, to be more precise. The question one must always ask about advertising is whether it is ethical to manipulate people, to get them to do certain things that you want them to do. Advertisers argue, of course, that they are relatively powerless and that what they do is provide information that people can first evaluate and then make up their own minds. It's an interesting exercise to turn off the sound and examine the images in a commercial—you'll see incredible use of body language; of facial expressions; of everything the actors and actresses can do to generate an emotional response in those who view these works. Advertising is not, for the most part, information; it is emotion!

In 1998 I was fortunate enough to win an award by the Advertising Education Foundation and spent three weeks at Goldberg Moser O'Neill, a large advertising agency in San Francisco, as a "visiting professor." Everyone was very nice to me and I learned a lot, wandering around and chatting with various people. They were, as a rule, very bright and hardworking, and kind to give me so much of their time.. There was, I could see, a mountain of labor behind every print ad or commercial.

One day I was chatting with Fred Goldberg, the number one honcho of the agency (now retired), and we were talking about an ad he was looking at in a newspaper. "It's a lousy ad," Fred said, "But the amazing thing is that even lousy ads work!" If even the lousy ads work, what hope do most people have of not being affected by them, especially since we are exposed to so many print ads and radio commercials and television commercials in the course of a given day? "It's a 260 billion dollar-a-year business," he said, "and most of the companies keep advertising because they hope that one day, somehow, they will get an agency to create a blockbuster ad for them that will turn everyone on. It's like playing the lottery. One company gave me hell about the amount of money we were spending on corned beef sandwiches on the shoot for a commercial we were making for them, but didn't think twice about signing the media bill for almost ten million dollars' worth of air time."

Some teenagers were asked by a researcher whether they were affected by advertising. "No," most of them said. "We're aware of advertising but we're not affected by it." Being deluded about one's behavior is not unique to teenagers, but the idea that teenagers aren't affected by advertising is similar, as far as truth values are concerned, to saying the earth is flat! Teenagers have hundreds of billions of dollars of discretionary income, and the advertising agencies make sure, as best they can, that teenagers and their money are soon parted.

American Studies

In 1960 I went off to the University of Minnesota to pursue a doctorate in American Studies. For a while it seemed that American Studies was the most exciting new development in universities—an interdisciplinary (or is it multi-disciplinary or pan-disciplinary?) program that enabled students to build a coherent course of study. In theory, one could investigate some topic of interest in terms of its social, psychological, political, literary (and other) aspects.

I had a wonderful time at the University of Minnesota. Unlike many of my colleagues, who hoped to teach literature, I was more interested in the social sciences and so I spent most of my time taking courses in American Intellectual History, Political Theory, and the Humanities than I did in Literature. I took many of my courses with David Noble, an intellectual historian, Mulford Sibley, a political theorist, and Ralph Ross, who taught in the Humanities department. I also took courses in American Music, in American Literature, and so on. These courses turned out to be very useful to me when I wrote my dissertation, under Mulford Sibley's direction, on the comic strip *Li'l Abner*. I always went for the best professor and didn't care too much about what he or she was teaching.

When I told my brother Jason, an artist, that I was going off to the University of Minnesota to study American Studies, he said it would be better to study one subject in depth. That argument, I must say, has been made by many academics, who think that people who study American Studies emerge as dilettantes, with a smattering of knowledge in this and in that. But there is nothing to say that a person can't design a program of courses that holds together and provides a better perspective on things than students who are in one discipline. Doesn't it make sense for someone who teaches American Literature to have studied American Political Thought, History, and other courses that provide a sense of context? At Minnesota there were some professors who formed the core of the program, but students could take courses from whoever they wanted—as long as their advisor thought their program of courses made sense.

I found American Studies to my liking. I was intellectually

curious and learned a great deal. I also made use of my ability to draw and did a number of illustrations for the Student American Studies Association, with which I was deeply involved. I might have run it for a few years. I developed a motto for our association:

> *"Two Years Before the Master's Degree, a Decade Before the Ph.D."*

I had smooth sailing through my written exams, but when I took my orals I ran into trouble with a professor who didn't agree with some of my ideas. A compromise was reached—I would write a few papers on Rousseau and some works of American literature and that would take care of the matter. I was heading off for a Fulbright in Italy and the committee gave me the benefit of the doubt about my performance in the orals. I was lucky, in a sense—in that the professors let me write the papers. But I was unlucky because if a different professor had been on my orals committee, I probably wouldn't have had any trouble at all.

UM BERTO   ECO

I went off to Milan for a year, where I met Umberto Eco and spent some time with him and his friends. Then I came back and wrote my dissertation and got a job at San Francisco State University. I had three offers: one at the University of Southern Florida, in Humanities; one at Southern Illinois, in Literature; and one at San Francisco State College (now University), in a small Social Science department. I chose San Francisco, for obvious reasons. It was the lesser of the institutions, but it was the one with the best location.

American Studies scholars, until recently, made up for their feelings of inadequacy and not being in a traditional discipline, like Literature or Sociology, by writing excruciatingly boring papers on dull and uninteresting subjects. Now that cultural studies has liberated scholars in the Social Sciences and Humanities, I would hope the papers in the American Studies journals won't be so nauseatingly vapid.

5

It was I who drove a knife deep into the heart of that castrating bitch...

A CONFESSION BY AGOSTINO GLIOMA

An Assassin of Academics

I am, I must confess, an assassin of academics. I've written a number of dark comic academic mysteries in which I've managed to kill, using various means—knives, poison, guns, poison arrows, bombs–a dozen or so professors and an occasional dean and college president. It is very therapeutic killing off professors and others involved in academia. In my mystery novels I also express the certain kind of ambivalence (or is it sadness or anger?) I feel about what is happening in universities nowadays as they become more and more corporatized.

Thus, in my comic mystery *Die Laughing*, I have my narrator, Agostino Glomma, a berserk professor from the University of California at Berkeley, speculate about academic life. He had murdered six professors in a previous book, *The Hamlet Case*, and has just been released from San Quentin Prison after doing his time.

In universities, one gets ahead by projecting an attitude of high seriousness and giving people the impression–often false, of course–that one is working on important matters. You have to develop a certain look–the look of a strategic thinker who is scanning the distant horizon for the newest ideas. You of course are thinking about screwing a beautiful co-ed in the fourth row of one of your classes but you seem to be struggling with enormous thoughts and weighty problems.

It helps if you can write in an unintelligible manner; the French are masters of this. I don't think anyone really understands what Baudrillard or Derrida or Foucault or DeLeuze writes. The more opaque and elliptical the better, and the more nonsense you write–with a sense of assurance and confidence to carry it all off–the higher your reputation will be. That is because academics, all of whom think they are brilliant and remarkable, will assume that since they can't figure out what you are talking about, you must be even more brilliant than they are. I always advise young faculty members to read the French philosophers and culture critics and imitate them stylistically.

If you publish very little, you explain that your work is theoretically important and that you are not a hack, like certain colleagues you could mention in your university, whose work is everywhere. You mention the term "public intellectual" with a sneer. It is quality, not quantity, that counts, you say. Your work, you suggest, has taken enormous thought and energy, and if it is not well received critically, it is because you are so far ahead of your time. Attitude is all in academia and you must convince those who dole out the money, the deans and the provosts, that you are one of their brightest stars.

The ultimate dream of university administrators, it seems, is to have a university with only administrators and students and maybe a handful of professors, at the most. The only problem is that a virtual professoriat teaching courses on the Internet would lead, ineluctably, to a virtual set of university administrators. University administrators want to avoid virtuality at all costs. In recent years they have been multiplying at an enormous rate. Professors, of course, would like to rid universities of administrators, who came to administer and take care of minor bureaucratic functions–parking and that sort of thing–and stayed to command.

I've been in universities for most of my adult life (I don't know whether I should be pitied or be given a medal for foolhardy valor). That is, I've been connected, as a student or a member of the faculty, with one university or another since 1950. I started as a student at the University of Massachusetts in Amherst in 1950, continued on as a student at the University of Iowa in Iowa City, "the Athens of the Midwest," from 1954 to 1956. Then there was an interruption of four years. I spent almost two years in the U.S. Army, and when I was released I went to Europe. I lived in Paris for around six months and then made a "grand tour" of Europe. I returned to the United States in 1959 and spent a year in New York City, working for a few months for a union newspaper.

Sat. Sept. 15, 2012 (overcast)

Danila and her husband took us to a very nice steak house... God only knows what it cost. They ordered a Filet Mignon for me... and two different kinds of steaks... We were there from 9:00 PM until 11:30 PM... I had a lot of wine. There and fell asleep immediately... around 12:30 AM... I slept and dozed until 7:30 AM...

Today's my last day in Buenos Aires... I'm off to La Plata tomorrow... everyone tells me how nice Rosario is... It's a city of around a million people... Today I will relax... I'm talking to P. at 1:00 o'clock.

I did a bit of work but was very tired and went back to bed and slept until 10:15 AM + I managed to answer a number of Vid hya's queries even before I return to Mill Valley... So there won't be much left for me to do except work on the index... I don't know what to make of the book... I'll see what kind of a response it gets from reviewers, users, etc... if any.

The mystery of my Bali Tourism remains... No bookshop have it and there are no copies on Internet bookstores... I guess it can be classified as a "stealth" publication... Routledge don't want anyone to know about it, or so it seems.

It's overcast so my clothes aren't drying as fast as they do when there's sun... but they'll be dry by this evening or tomorrow at the latest. Then I'll have six days in La Plata... but I've got four pairs of underpants and eight pairs of socks... and three or four tee shirts + two long sleeved shirts, etc etc.

I went out for a walk... went on some different streets but I could see there's little difference from one street to the next... on the main drag, Avenida Santa Fe, isn't that industry that I may take a nap soon... I've been tired from the pace of activities.

I had another nap this afternoon... I must be run down from the pace here. It's going to rain for the next few days I believe from watching the TV news... doesn't look good... So I'll be in my hotel

And then I went to the University of Minnesota in Minneapolis, from 1960 to 1965. In 1963-1964, I had a Fulbright grant and taught at the University of Milan. In 1965, I joined the faculty of San Francisco State University and was there until I retired in 2003, except for a year in 1984 at the University of Southern California in Los Angeles when I taught a course on Popular Culture at the Annenberg School for Communication.

In America the term "academic" has rather negative connotations. We tend to contrast academics with the people in the "real" world, with people who are practical, with people who can "cope." Academics are supposed to be unworldly—all caught up in their particular interests which are often esoteric and petty and seem to have little value or utility. Americans are supposedly anti-intellectual and scornful of academics, but they, for the most part, want their children to go to the best universities and get a good education...if only because it is now necessary to have a college education to get a decent job.

The lengths to which some parents, and young people, go to get into the best universities are now quite absurd. Sometimes parents start the process of trying to get their children into Harvard in the third grade. One person I know had his son study the bassoon, since he figured that the Harvard symphony orchestra would need bassoon players. It worked! His son did get into Harvard and went there. My son did also. "My Harvard years were," as he used to put it, "the happiest years of my mother's life."

Although I've spent most of my life in universities, I've never really been comfortable in them. My older brother Jason, who taught painting at various art schools in Boston (and for a year in Buffalo), also had trouble with academic institutions. The Berger brothers, on both coasts, never quite fit in with academia.

I now obtain a good deal of pleasure by writing comic academic murder mysteries that also generally deal with some topic, such as Postmodernism or ways of interpreting *Hamlet* or mass communication theory. If you're going to be a disgruntled professor, you should find a way to make it pay off, I say. For example, I wrote a mystery, *Postmortem for a Postmodernist* (AltaMira Press), that explains different perspectives on Postmodernism. In this mystery, a professor from the University of California at Berkeley, Ettore Gnocchi, is killed four different ways on the first page.

G. Gorer ⊗ Themes in Japanese Culture (1943)	A Sea Mystique p 52/53 on Geats	John Gunther Inside Asia Harper + BMS. NY 1939	GEISHAS Number of not prostitutes
AMAE "dependency on the benevolence + kindness of others"	8', 000 geishas in 1965 to 1695 in Tokyo	SANJA MATSURI Eric Cohen authenticity	Description of 1 service studio general false ideas about Japanese culture
Power Japan	mapiko :	POMO	relation to macho
Several yrs t ? the Japanese — John Gunther	Elements of Japanese in Inside Asia , 000	Partly Absolute Irony Seclusion Japan contemptuous + doubtless	symbol of Japaneseness
Religion on philosophy + Tao	Geisha and Seclusion	Subcultures have drawn support	Asian woman mystique
The "real" Japan + architecture	SANJA 750 MATSURI who Festival	Breakdown of Codes of Conduct belief + behaviour	"old Japan" 6th v3. New Japan
GEISHAS + macho MATSURI 2000	down side of with tourism	Breakdown Dissolution of social order	"sugar girls" expensive men places
Japan as a POSTMODERN Country	authenticity + ancient Festival other side of "proposed" Japanese culture	New form of Capitalism and Tourism	Tere Travel with Geishas Regression. Nostalgia for earlier qualities true
Fendel / Modern Nationalism Consumer Culture + Materialism	Religion Ritual + Scholarly	Freedom — had odd jobs	Exotic + Erotic
	Japanese very carnival	SHINJINRUI The new poor	Erotic. differentness Sex Tourism sordid those
ASAKUSA FESTIVAL	Borders of the carnivalesque	under 30 wild clothes colored hair	What makes found in
Gem Society on "chanting" schmog	Sense of exaltation — The air — anticipation of Seeing a great of young + women camps relics	Individual class in a group centred culture	Items over 1 item em 794 – 1185
Number of Gangs in Japan	3rd weekend of May Shinto Festival	G.d - Gang Theory on Japan ?? Shelonge — hub of Shogunate	Came from china
SANJA Soma matsuri festival MATSURI	3rd Sunday + preceding Friday, Sat in May Nikko Portable Shrine Japanese to elements	Shitsuge Gods greatest comfort free spending youths of aristocrats	"cool" hand pulled born in a lum

I have the pages in my journals in which I got the idea for writing *Postmortem for a Postmodernist* and did some planning for the book. I was speculating about courses I was teaching or might be teaching when an image popped into my head—of someone with his head on a table, who had been shot in the head, had a poison arrow in his cheek, a knife in his back and had spilled a drink that had poison in it.

It was Feb. 25, 1996.

Then I devoted part of a page to doing some plotting. It was one things to figure out what to write in the first chapter, which was very short. I had to figure out where to go from the first chapter.

So this book started with an image and then I spent time working out the plot in my journals Most of my books started in my journals. I'd play around with an idea and then when I had something that I thought had possibilities, I'd do some brainstorming and eventually worked out the plots of the mysteries and the topics for chapters in my nonfiction books.

In another one of my mysteries, *The Mass Comm Murders: Five Media Theorists Self Destruct* (Rowman & Littlefield) I deal with mass communication theory. In this mystery, five media theorists kill one another off. In my mystery *The Hamlet Case* (Xlibris), I have my hero (or is it villain) Agostino Glioma kill off six professors, but not before each of them has offered a different interpretation of *Hamlet.*They were all members of the editorial board of the journal he edited, *Shakespeare Studies,* and he was afraid they were going to replace him as editor. He also plays a part in my mystery *Die Laughing,* which is about different approaches to humor.

The most important thing about my academic career, as far as I am concerned, is that it gave me the time and freedom to pursue my scholarly interests and write my books. Many professors mistakenly argue that the three best things about academic life are, sad to say—June, July and August! They are, of course, forgetting about the month between semesters!

Aristotle's Lost Book on Comedy

One of my books I published with Xlibris, an Internet print-on-demand publisher, is a pseudo-translation of Aristotle's "lost book" on comedy. It is the first literary hoax I've written (some would claim all my books are hoaxes). I am, I must confess, something of a trickster and put-on artist, and I've had a lot of fun, over the last forty years, in that role. So I imagine it isn't too surprising that I perpetrate a literary hoax.

My idea was to pretend to discover and then to translate and annotate Aristotle's famous "lost" book on comedy. He mentions this book in his writings but nobody has ever seen it and there is a question about whether Aristotle never got around to writing it or whether he wrote it but it has been lost. I took the latter tack and parodying his style, to the extent that I was able, I wrote a book (actually a long article) in which I claimed to have discovered Aristotle's lost book on humor and translated it from the Greek, with numerous annotations.

What I did, actually, was take a glossary on the forty-five techniques of humor that I had elicited in some research I did many years ago (and written about in my books *An Anatomy of Humor and The Art of Comedy Writing*) and using Aristotle's "voice," have him explain most of these techniques. To flesh out the book (and some of Aristotle's books are relatively short, you should understand), I annotated my fake Aristotle and offered various jokes and other material relevant to the study of humor. When I did this I still had only about forty pages of manuscript- -I needed to figure out a way to get a book-length manuscript. So I added a comic mystery, "The Aristotle Case," in which the board members of "The International Aristotle Society" (which I invented., though there probably are groups like it) had a panel at a meeting of the Modern Language Association to discuss the authenticity of the translation. I also put myself on the panel. One of the members is murdered and an investigation ensues.

In the investigation, interestingly enough, I am interviewed by my detective.

I had my typical international cast of characters: male and female professors from England, from Russia, from Germany, from Italy, and France...each of whom is involved with one another in complicated ways– love affairs, broken love affairs, as well as different perspectives on Aristotle. I use them to spoof stereotypes people have about people from different countries. And I used my detective, one Solomon Hunter, who has been in most of my mysteries, to solve the murder.

Dramatis Personae

Yves-Marie Fess.
A Freudian critic at the University of Paris X, he specializes in the study of Aristotle and humor from a psychoanalytic perspective. His book on Aristotle, *The Aristotelian Unconscious*, was considered by many an important contribution, and his book on comedy, The Laughing Assassin, had been well reviewed. He is secretary of the International Aristotle Society.

Marlena Kugel.
She is professor of philosopher at the University of Berlin who teaches Aristotelian philosophy. She is the author of *Aristotle- -Our Contemporary*, which argues that Aristotle was the first postmodernist philosopher. She is treasurer of the International Aristotle Society.

Anastasia Pelmenyi-Irkutsk.
Anastasia Pelmenyi-Irkutsk, is a Marxist political scientist at the University of California at Berkeley and the director of the Institute for Contemporary Marxist Philosophy. Among her many books are Aristotle's Marx and *Is Man a Political Animal?*. She received her doctorate from the University of Moscow, writing on Aristotle's influence on Marx. She is program director for the International Aristotle Society.

Contessa Allesandra Mirabella-Grappa.
She is a semiotician who teaches at the University of Bologna, even though she lives in Milan. Her book, *Aristotle as Sign* deals with his theory from a semiotic perspective and her book Laughing at Signs, is considered a seminal contribution to the semiotic theory of humor. She is editor of Aristotle, the official journal of the International Aristotle Society.

Sir Humbert House.

Sir Humbert House, M.A. (Oxon), Regius Professor of Classics at the University of Oxford, is a world renowned authority on Greek thought, and the author of twenty three books on Aristotle, Greek culture and similar topics.. His book, *Aristotle's Sense of Humor*, attempts to offer an Aristotelian theory of humor based on his writings in Rhetoric, Poetics, and other works . He is president of the International Aristotle Society.

Arthur Asa Berger.

An author, from the San Francisco area, of numerous books on popular culture and humor, Berger claims to have found Aristotle's so-called "lost book" on humor, *Comedy*. Berger asserts that he translated *Comedy* from the Greek and also annotated it. This translation of Aristotle was the subject of an eagerly anticipated panel, to determine its authenticity, at the Modern Language Association meetings in San Francisco held in July 18-21, 2000, at the Hilton hotel. The board of directors of the International Aristotle Society had gathered to deal with the issue.

In this book I also did something I'd always thought about— have one or two lines of textual material and the rest of the page filled with a footnote. The first page of my translation and annotation of Aristotle's lost book, Comedy, follows:

> [Translator's Note: Aristotle's words are shown in regular type and *my annotations are shown in italics.*]
>
> Comedy, like Epic poetry, Tragedy, and Dithirambic poetry, is a mode of imitation that is a dramatic picture of the ridiculous.
>
> *The concept of imitation is of central importance in Aristotle's theory of art. He argues that art is an imitation of life. Mimesis is the Greek term for imitation and thus Aristotle believes that art is an imitation or mirror, if you will, of life.*
>
> *There are other theorists who argue that art doesn't mirror life but projects its own reality–that is, art is closer to being a lamp, to use a term from M.H. Abrams. Some theorists argue that art should be understood as having a mission, as being useful for doing certain things–the*

pragmatic theory of art. Finally, there are theorists who argue that art exists to give us kicks, to create new sensations in people.

Ever since Aristotle's time, people have been arguing about what art is and what it does and what it should do. Many people nowadays, without realizing it, accept Aristotle's mimetic theory of art and judge works of art by how faithful they are to our so-called reality. In our contemporary postmodern world, however, the mimetic theory art doesn't appeal to many people who tend to fudge the difference between art and non-art or reality.

There is also the question of what imitation means… and the ontological status of imitations. Is margarine an imitation of butter or is it something real on its own. Does something that starts as an imitation become, somehow, real. And can something that's an imitation become, in people's minds, more real than real. Consider motion pictures, for example. For many people they are more real than so-called "real life." There are some theorists who switch things around and argue that life is an imitation of art.

Because this is a rather eccentric book and I didn't think any regular publisher would be interested in it, I decided to publish with it Xlibris.com. Until February 28, 2001 you could actually publish books with Xlibris at no cost. That is, Xlibris would design the cover and set the book into type, using the file you sent them on a diskette.. Then, Xlibris would print copies of the book, one at a time, as orders came in. After February 28, 2001, the cost for books went to $200, so I made certain I got the manuscript in before that date.

These books that Xlibris and IUniverse publish are listed at Amazon.com and BarnesandNoble.com and are printed on demand, thanks to new developments in printing technology. I don't believe it will be an electronic book, that people can download and read on computers (I might be wrong about this), but it will be a book that looks like any other book. The staff at Xlibris actually did a decent job with the cover, too.

I don't know how many people other than myself will order copies of the book. Like all authors, I feel that if a book is available someone *may* order it, and that's what's important. There's always a chance that a book will catch on.

I must report a bit of fun I had with my Aristotle book. I saw on the Internet that an electronic journal was looking for articles that mixed genres, so I sent them a half dozen pages of the Aristotle "comedy." My thought was that I had a bit of fiction (the so-called translation of the "lost book" on comedy) and a bit of fact—my annotations. I received an e-mail back saying that the judges thought that while my translation of Aristotle was fine, nobody could see how I was blending or mixing genres. They didn't realize that my translation was a hoax and pretended that they were able to evaluate my "translation" of Aristotle from the Greek. I got a big kick out of that.

Army Days

Certification of
Military Service

This certifies that   Arthur A. Berger

was a member of the   Army of the United States

from   July 12, 1956

to   May 15, 1958

Service was terminated by   Honorable Release from Active Duty

Last Grade, Rank, or Rating   Specialist Third Class

Active Service Dates   Same As Above

Date of Birth: Not Available   Place of Birth: Not Available

Given at St. Louis, Missouri on December 30, 2014

Eleven days after I got my master's degree in journalism from the University of Iowa, I was in the United States Army. I had been drafted! I was twenty-three at the time and thought that the Army would be looking for younger men, but I was wrong. I was released from the Army in May 15, 1958, several months before my two years were up. It was, at the time, the happiest day of my life.

I served my basic training at Fort Hood, Texas, in the infantry. I can remember that by 8:00 AM, the water in my canteen was hot. Basic training certainly was one of the most horrendous experiences I've ever had, and I'd probably still be in Fort Hood, on the firing range, trying to amass the requisite number of points to be allowed off the range, if my Captain hadn't asked a young recruit, who shot well, to pretend to be me. He was semi-literate but he knew how to shoot straight. I emerged from the firing range with a black eye and a swollen lip and with little ability to fire a rifle and hit a target…or anything.

Somehow, the captain who was in charge of us, Captain Huff, discovered that I was an artist. He discovered this because I let it be known to various sergeants and officers in my outfit (I discovered in the course of my career in the army that, curiously, artists get a great deal of respect). Once this happened, my life changed considerably. I was assigned the task of painting my company's insignia on a large rock in front of the headquarters building of my outfit. I managed to stretch the job out into days. I could have done it in an hour if I pushed myself. I can recall working on the rock and listening to the captain talking with his Lieutenants.

"What the hell are we supposed to do with them?" he asked.

17

The problem was that my outfit had done everything it was supposed to do, and there were days and days left before we were to be shipped off.

"Let's march the fuckers," said a lieutenant, and that's what they did—back and forth, back and forth, under the blazing sun. People were passing out left and right. While this was happening, I was taking my own good time painting the rock. Even more important, I also requisitioned a big jar full of ice water. Somehow the army recognized that artists had to be treated in special ways. I then convinced our captain that it would be good for morale if we had a newspaper for our outfit, and explained to him that I had a master's degree in journalism. And so I spent the last days of my basic training writing a newspaper to improve morale. It was called "Charlie's Chuckles."

After eight weeks of basic training I emerged a "trained killer" and was shipped off to Washington, D.C., where I was sent to a small public relations outfit at a place called Cameron Station. I ended up being declared "surplus" there and was destined to be sent to Fort Belvoir, a base thirty or forty miles from Washington, D.C. It didn't look good.

So one afternoon I went to building T-7, an adjunct of the Pentagon, where the public information office of the Military District of Washington was located. The Colonel who ran the office, Colonel George Creel, was away. He was the son of a very famous General. But his assistant, a lieutenant colonel, Lieutenant Colonel Nicholas, was there and interviewed me. He was interested in getting me for his office, but he didn't have the clout to do so, being only a Lieutenant Colonel (in the Pentagon, two star generals get coffee for three star Generals). While I was sitting in the office, a big, strapping fellow came in—a Major—and asked the secretary, "Is anyone here an artist? I've got to make a chart to brief the old man." The "old man" was the Major General who ran the Military District of Washington, Major General Lesley Van Houten.

"I'm sorry," said the secretary. "Nobody here's an artist."

"Excuse me, Major," I volunteered. "I happen to be an artist."

"Okay," he said, "Come with me."

He led me down the hallway to his office. He had a big piece of white cardboard and he wanted me to draw someone in a parachute, and then have me print something beneath it.

"Not only can I draw the parachutist, I can draw you as the parachutist," I said. It so happens that at the University of Iowa I used to make money going to dances and drawing caricatures of people for a dollar a drawing.

"Great!" he said.

I sat him down and started drawing a caricature of him.

"Who are you?" he asked. "I don't recall seeing you around here."

"I'm trying to get a spot in the public information office, sir," I said.

"I was declared surplus at Cameron Station and I'm going to be sent down to Fort Belvoir. Lieutenant Colonel Nicholas would like to get me, because I have a master's degree in Journalism, but he doesn't have enough clout, and the head of the office, Colonel Creel, is away. So it looks like I'm going down to Fort Belvoir."

I finished the caricature and printed in the text he wanted. He was overjoyed.

"A master's degree in Journalism," he said. "Like hell you're going to Fort Belvoir," he said. "I'm going in to see the old man right now, and you're going to be coming here. Wait here for a few minutes!"

With that he got up and left. Five minutes later he returned.

"It's all taken care of. I spoke to General Van Houten. You'll be taken down to Fort Belvoir and will stay there a few days. Then you'll be reassigned here, to the Military District of Washington. There isn't an opening in the public information office right now, so you'll be assigned to G-2. But you'll be moved to PIO as soon as something opens up."

19

A few days later I found myself in building T-7 in Washington, D.C., and at Fort Myers, and shortly after that in a beautiful fort in Washington, D.C., where five Generals lived and five Master Sergeants, along with a platoon of infantry (in another building).

"Congratulations," said Timothy Irving Murphy, who was in the bunk next to the one I was assigned, "you've just left the United States Army." We all worked in building T-7, so every morning we hopped on a bus and were taken there. And we were paid extra to buy our lunches there. In the afternoon, we took the bus back. We also had one afternoon off every week.

I was temporarily assigned to G2, where I worked on maps.

When Colonel Creel came back and found out about me, and that I was in G-2, he was afraid the Colonel in charge of G-2 wouldn't let me go, so Creel used his brains. He bet him a dollar that he wouldn't release me. Creel knew that the colonel in charge of G-2 loved to win bets. Eventually, a few weeks later, Creel lost his bet, and I was transferred to the public information office where I became a feature writer. In my office we had graduates of Yale, Harvard, Princeton, Amherst, Brown and me— from Iowa.

It only cost Colonel Creel one dollar to get me. I wrote speeches for the General, I ghosted articles from our officers, and I took care of other matters like calling the White House every morning to see which political figures were coming to Washington, D.C., so I could send out notices to the press. I ghosted an article for Lt. Colonel Nicholas on the Pentagon that was widely praised. Creel told me I did a great job with it.

I got out of the Army several months early by a stroke of luck. The Master Sergeant who ran our office was on leave…I think he was taking exams for a master's degree at one of the universities in Washington, D.C. I had done a good deal of art work for various officers in my building and had their good will. It turns out that you could only get out of the Army early if you had a seasonal job—like being a farmer. I had a friend with a summer camp in Switzerland. I got him to send me a letter saying I had a job there—at International Ranger Camp in Glion sur Montreux, Switzerland, starting in June.

So when I told one of the officers who was in charge of such things that I wanted to get out of the Army several months early to start on a career as a camp counselor and showed him the letter, he had a good laugh, but he signed my early release form. I was to be released May 15, 1958. When the Master Sergeant came back from his leave and found out I was getting out early, he hit the roof. But there was nothing he could do.

In addition, I found out that the dentist who took care of Eisenhower was at Walter Reed hospital. It turns out that I had a molar that had grown in sideways under my gum and knew that one day I'd have to have it out. A month before I was to be released, I went to Walter Reed and said my tooth was hurting me. They took an x-ray and saw the molar down there beneath my gum. The dentist, the one that treated Eisenhower, had a team of dentists that went around with him. One of them said to me, "No problem. Easy to treat."

A date was scheduled for my surgery. The operation ended up taking three hours—they had to break the molar into three pieces and take them out one at a time. My face swelled up like a balloon, and I spent the next three weeks in bed, reading travel books and going back and forth to Walter Reed to have my dentist see how I was doing.

Every enlisted man in the Army is a schemer, seeking ways to make his life easier and less burdensome, trying to get a better deal for himself. I was no different from anyone else. Every day in the Army I felt like a prisoner...perhaps because I was one. On paper the Army looks marvelous: everything is worked out logically. But because the Army is full of all kinds of bizarre types with a genius for screwing things up, all kinds of crazy things happen. At least I escaped alive and not too brain-damaged from my twenty-one months in the Army.

I wouldn't wish it on anyone. And yet, there was a certain sense of comradeship that I felt with some of my "buddies" that was quite marvelous.

One day I was asked to show some sports reporters from *The Washington Post* around the Pentagon.

"How did you end up in the Army?" one of them asked me.

"I has just got my masters in journalism from the University of Iowa, and the next thing I knew I was drafted," I said.

"You've got a degree in journalism?" his colleague asked.

"Yes," I replied.

"Listen, we need some people to help us in the sports department on the weekends. You interested?"

"Sure," I said.

And so I became a weekend high school sports reporter for *The Washington Post*. The sports reporters there were the wildest guys I've ever met...often, around midnight, after we took care of our work ("putting the paper to bed," as they put it), they would drag me off to parties or to the Press Club, where we would play pool and drink beer until 5:00 AM. Many of them were married and had kids. I don't know how they did it (it was the money I made from *The Washington Post* and saved from the Army that financed my year in Europe).

One thing I learned from the Army that it is important to look busy. So I typed letters to my friends when I had no work to do—so I'd be occupied with something. If I weren't, someone would find something for me to do. And when I went out of my office, I always carried a piece of paper with something typed on it so it would seem that I was doing something.

The best piece of paper I ever carried in my career in the U.S. Army was the one releasing me from service on May 15th.

Arthur Asa

I happen to be a Bostonian, which means I don't pronounce my "R's," so I always have a lot of trouble telling people my name, and some people have come away from phone calls with me thinking my name is "Otto." Other people kid me about my Bostonian pronunciation, and many people call me "Athuh."

Sometimes my wife asks me what I'd call myself if I decided to change my first name. My daughter, born Miriam Frances Berger, changed her name and now is Nina Savelle. When she married, she began to call herself Nina Savelle Rocklin. She changed it when she was an aspiring actress and thought it had more panache, I imagine. The Savelle is a modification of my mother's maiden name, Savel. I had an uncle, born Jacob Savel, who used to call himself Jackson Gregory Savelle, thinking it suggested someone English and aristocratic.

Names have a certain significance in the scheme of things. Arthur doesn't suggest romance or glamor. One thinks of waiters or servants or chauffeurs named Arthur, not heroes. There was one heroic Arthur, King Arthur, but he's from ancient history. Children aren't named Arthur very often nowadays. They have names like Noah or Tyler or Brennan. The pianist Arthur Rubinstein dropped the "h" in his name and became Artur Rubinstein, which suggested someone from Europe and had more dash to it. I would say the same applies to Arturo.

So I've spent my life with a rather unexciting first name. However, my middle name, Asa, has a touch of mystery about

it. Asa is very unusual. Some of my colleagues at San Francisco State call me Asa—they don't know I have a first name, I imagine. Asa has, I think, an image that goes with it… a very old Yankee, a geezer, perhaps in a Brooks Brothers suit. One of my friends, Aaron Wildavsky, always called me "Arthur Asa," to separate me, I imagine, from all the other Arthurs he knew. I used my middle name because there was another Arthur Berger—Arthur Victor Berger—who was an academic and taught at Brandeis, and who I met many years ago… I wanted to make sure my books weren't confused with his. What's really curious is that even now many people call me by my middle name and I get e-mail messages addressed to Asa Berger. For years I hated my middle name; now, I think, it might be well to drop my first name.

When I lived in Italy, sometimes I would take my young daughter to a park, where she would play with little boys with names like "Herculeo, Ulysses, and Giuseppe." Giuseppe" means "Joseph," and, is almost as plebeian as Arthur. Giuseppe Verdi means Joseph Green in English. Not very exciting! I can only wonder what kind of a life I'd have led if my mother had named me Arturo instead of Arthur. Or Rodney.

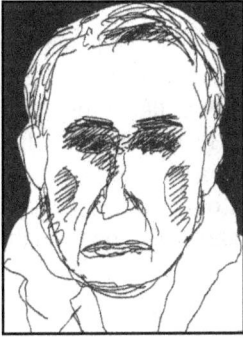

Barthes

When I read Roland Barthes' *Mythologies*, I felt a wonderful sense of vindication and relief. For here was Roland Barthes, one of France's most influential intellectuals, writing a book about life in France, and what did he write about? Wrestling! Garbo's Face! Steak and Chips! Toys! Striptease! Is that the kind of thing one expects from a world-famous scholar? What's going on here? Mythologies reminded me, in a way, of McLuhan's marvelous, and underappreciated, book *The Mechanical Bride*, which treated print advertisements and comics, among other things, as signs to be decoded.

Barthes explains, in the preface to his 1970 edition, that he was offering "an ideological critique bearing on the language of so-called mass-culture," which was occasioned by his reading Saussure's book on semiology. "I had just read Saussure and as a result acquired the conviction that by treating 'collective representations' as sign-systems, one might hope to go further than the pious show of unmasking them and account *in detail* for the mystification which transforms petite-bourgeois culture into a universal nature."

Barthes wrote the essays in *Mythologies* one per month between 1954 and 1956 "on topics suggested by current events." Each essay was an attempt to strip away the mystification from important aspects of French life, for each of his topics was accepted as that "which goes without saying," and he was trying to show that this naturalness was cultural and as result of the way the media presented things to the French public.

I had been trying to do the same thing long before I had read Barthes or McLuhan because I sensed, like them, that it is in our common places that one can tease out the elements of our fundamental beliefs. We may not be conscious of these beliefs or be able to articulate them, if asked. But people in most cultures learn certain core principles that guide their thoughts and behavior, and it was these hidden or covert aspects of culture that I've always been after.

Barthes wrote a similar book in his *Empire of Signs*, except that his book dealt with Japanese culture. He isolated a number of topics that he thought were important—Japanese chopsticks, stationery stores, tempura...it is from topics like these that Barthes presented his picture of Japan. He pointed out that he was not offering a portrait, a coherent and unified study of Japanese culture, but, instead, a discussion of certain aspects of Japanese culture that struck his attention and which he thought had resonance and significance.

When I read McLuhan and Barthes and Saussure, it was as if a dark veil was lifted from my eyes. I instinctively felt that many so-called "trivial" matters, like wrestling (about which I'd written) and comic strips (I've written two books about comics and a number of articles about them) and McDonald's hamburgers (I wrote an article on it titled *The Evangelical Hamburger*) were really of considerable importance—if one could learn how to read them. Saussure provided the theory and McLuhan and Barthes the examples, and some theory, that set me on my course.

I wrote one book, *Bloom's Morning*, that did the same kind of thing Barthes did in *Mythologies* except my book had a narrative line to it and was tied much more to everyday life's domestic routines.

Bloom's Morning

The day my book *Bloom's Morning* was published I started believing in miracles. I say that because it is a somewhat strange little book and though I came close to getting it published a few times, I eventually concluded, reluctantly, that nobody would ever publish it.

My original title for the book was *Ulysses Sociologica*. What I planned to do in the book was take one day in the life of a typical American, who I named Bloom, and examine, from an anthropological and sociological point of view, all the different objects he used and rituals he went through. That is, I would take James Joyce's *Ulysses* as a model and write a sociological (in the broadest sense) study of everyday life in America.

I got the idea in the early seventies, and have numerous places in my journals where I speculate about how such a book might be written and what I might deal with. In 1982 or thereabouts I bought a computer—a Commodore 64—for $900. I thought my son Gabriel might become interested in computers but he never took to them—until recently, that is, and now he works as a senior engineer for a computer company. I also had, for the first time, a very elemental word processing system.

I decided, then, that I would learn how to use the word processing program by writing *Ulysses Sociologica*, and so, over the next month and a half, I wrote something like thirty-five essays, on topics I had decided were important signifiers of American culture and values. I had set a number of pages aside in my journal and listed the topics I might deal with... and brainstormed on each of them. It was very difficult work because for my book to work I had to discover something interesting and surprising about each of my topics—whether it was the clock-radio, which was my first topic, or toasters or gel toothpaste or slippers or trash compactors, which were other topics I wrote about.

I also did a drawing for each topic I wrote about. Over the course of time I revised the essays a bit, but not substantially. I later turned them into a little book, based on pasting the illustrations on the top of a page and pasting the text I had written for a given topic beneath it. I duplicated twenty-five copies

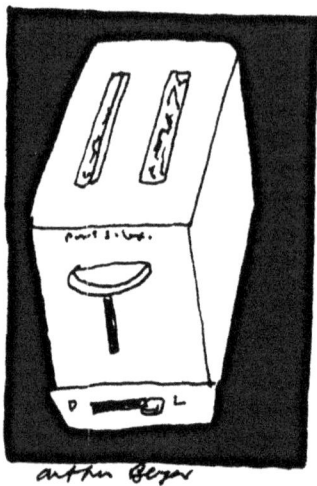

and had a "book," so to speak. Over the course of a number of years I found two or three editors who were interested in the book and liked it, but who could never convince their publishing committees (read marketing directors?) to allow them to publish the book. So I despaired of publishing it.

In the early nineties, I saw a notice that Douglas Kellner, a philosophy professor at the University of Texas, was editing a series on contemporary culture. I sent him a query about my book and he said he'd like to see it. I sent it to him, and he informed me that he would like to publish the book. But he had to get an editor at the publishing house that was doing the series to accept it. That editor said he found the book interesting, but he thought I should write an introduction to the book and a conclusion. So, I wrote an introduction on the theory of everyday life, and I wrote a conclusion about myth, culture and everyday life. The editor kept it for six or eight months and then rejected it. It's not unusual, I should point out, for editors to keep a book manuscript for months—even years—and then reject it.

God, I thought, *I'll never again come this close to getting Bloom's Morning published.* And so I reluctantly concluded, once again, that the book would never be published.

Then, in 1995 or 1996, someone told me that there was a very creative editor—a poet, actually—at Westview Press in Colorado named Gordon Massman. I sent him a query and he said he'd like to see the book. I sent it to him and he called and told me he loved the book. He said that when other people at Westview mentioned it, they started rolling their eyes.

I had sent him a printout of the manuscript, so he didn't see the drawings. I told him about them and he told me to send them to him right away. They made a huge difference. Once they saw my drawings, he told me, his colleagues at Westview

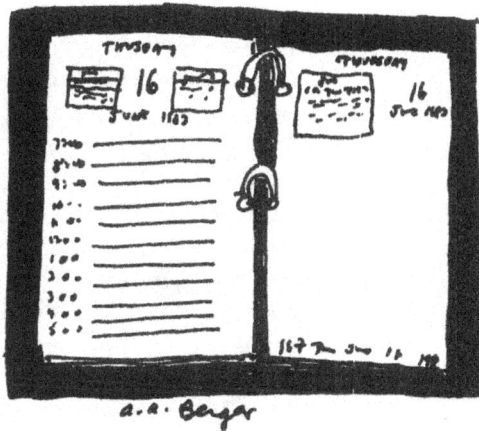

a.a. Berger

decided they loved the book, and Gordon was able to convince the editorial committee to publish it.

I can remember how excited I was the afternoon he called. I still couldn't believe that it would get published. Something will happen, I kept telling myself. I also did a drawing for the cover and some other drawings—of Freud and Joyce—for the introduction. I put Freud in because I adopted a technique of his from his book on dreams. In one place he recounts a dream and then takes every part of the dream and analyzes it. I did the same with my book, and so my first chapter was "Bloom's Morning." It reads as follows:

> *Mr. Leopold Bloom was awakened by the buzzer in his digital clock radio. He was lying on a king-sized bed in the master bedroom of his house. He lay beneath a designer sheet and a comforter, which he tossed aside, and slid out of bed. He was wearing a pair of pajamas. The broadloom carpet in the bedroom felt soft and comfortable. He put on his slippers and went to the closet where he took out his jogging outfit and got into it. He went for a job around the neighborhood, returned, got undressed, put on a bathrobe, and ambled over to the bathroom. He took a long, hot, invigorating shower. He loved the smell of the new bath soap he had purchased recently. He shampooed his hair. Then he put on his bathrobe again and dried his hair with an electric hairdryer. Next he b rushed his teeth using an electric toothbrush, took a shave, and put on his*

29

underwear. Then he put on his stockings, a suit, and his shoes, selecting a tie to wear, and went to the kitchen.

There wasn't much in the refrigerator, so he slipped out of the house and strolled to the local supermarket, where he picked up a few items, and returned home. The morning newspaper had arrived. He made himself a big breakfast: orange juice, cereal, bacon and eggs, coffee, and toast. He put his garbage in the waste disposal, his dirty dishes in the dishwasher, and an empty cereal carton in the trash compactor and hear the pleasant sound of the morning mail being slipped through the front door. That was Bloom's morning.

In my book I analyze the various objects mentioned and rituals engaged in by Bloom.

I had written the book assuming it would be sold as a scholarly book that might be adopted in courses on American culture or the sociology of everyday life in universities. Instead, for some reason, it was marketed as a trade book. That meant that three months after *Bloom's Morning* was published, it died. It was remaindered and that seemed to be the end of the story.

Not quite. It turns out that IUniverse.com has a program of reprinting books that are out of print, so now *Bloom's Morning* is available, on a print-on-demand basis, from IUniverse.com. I don't know whether it is correct to say that my Leopold Bloom still lives; perhaps it is more accurate to say that he exists in a kind of limbo, in a state of radical potentiality, waiting to be brought back to life by anyone who might find his story worth examining and who has fifteen dollars.

Publisher's Weekly's review of the book concluded as follows:

"Using toasters and supermarkets as springboards, Berger mounts a devastating critique of the increasingly impersonal, dehumanized quality of our lives."

Some reviewers considered the book far-fetched and silly while others loved it. My thought is that if I've mounted a devastating critique of American consumer culture and alienation with Bloom, he did not live in vain. And Bloom lives on elsewhere, too—my book has been translated into German and, of all things, into Chinese.

Cancer (A Slight Case of)

I have what might be described as a *slight* case of cancer—to the extent that any cancer can be seen as slight—aside from some skin cancers that are caught early. I discovered I had cancer in the fall of 1997. I had come back from participating in a workshop on humor at the University of Central Oklahoma and had a bad cold. I went to see my Internist, Dr. Goldman, at the Kaiser Foundation in San Rafael and he checked me over and suggested I wait a while and see what happened. When I didn't get better I went to him again and he had me take a blood test. He thought I might be anemic.

Several days later he called and in an excited voice told me that they had found something serious in the test and that I was to take some kind of a bone scan and see a new doctor, a hematologist…a woman named Dr. Krista Muirhead.

I called the nuclear medicine laboratory at the Kaiser hospital to inquire about the test.

"Are you being tested for osteoporosis or for cancer?" asked the technician.

When I heard that word I almost collapsed. Cancer! It was as if all the wind had been sucked out of my sails. This, from out of the blue.

Later Dr. Goldman called. My bone test suggested I didn't have Multiple Myeloma, which was good news, as news about one's cancer goes.

Several weeks later I had my appointment with Dr. Muirhead, who had just recently gone to work for the Kaiser foundation. I went with my wife, Phyllis. We were both scared. Dr. Muirhead was an attractive woman in her mid-thirties, I estimated. She smiled at us, shook our hands, and then told me that they weren't sure what I had, but it probably was something called Waldenstrom's Macroglobulemia or it might be Multiple Myeloma. Later she added Low-Grade Lymphoma (and eventually she said that low-grade lymphoma was probably what I had). She said they are incurable diseases but that they might not manifest themselves for ten or fifteen years. That was comforting.

"The median number of years before our discovery of low-grade lymphoma in people and their death is ten years," she told me. Several weeks later we went to the University of California at San Francisco Medical School for a second opinion—with a doctor with whom Dr. Muirhead had studied. He indicated that she had called him about my case. He looked at my x-rays and other material from Kaiser and said "You have ten years to live." That was, I found, less comforting. I was sixty-four and would have a rendezvous with destiny at seventy-four. That's about the age my father was when he died.

So we went to the Stanford University Medical School to see a world famous oncologist, Dr. Ronald Levy. We wanted a third opinion and my wife's medical plan covered my going there. He took my x-rays and other material from the Kaiser and disappeared. His assistant came in to talk with me for a few minutes and then also disappeared. After twenty minutes, Dr. Levy came back with his assistant. "He convinced me you have low-grade lymphoma," Dr. Levy said, "but it isn't certain. Your doctor didn't do a test that would have enabled us to be certain." After he left, his assistant, Dr. John Timmerman said, "Don't worry…something else will kill you before your lymphoma does." That was enormously comforting in a strange way. When you have cancer you can understand why.

Since then, I've lived my life more or less as I always did, though I don't have the energy I once had…and there's always that black cloud I live under. Every time I read the newspaper and see that someone has died from lymphoma, I cringe. But there are many different kinds of lymphoma and I have one that is very slow acting. I have a blood test every four months. Several weeks after the test I go to see Dr. Muirhead, who looks at the figures on my blood test and examines my lymph glands. Then she send me on my way. So far, I'm okay, and haven't needed any medication. If I have my choice, I'll take Dr. Timmerman's opinion and hope that something else will kill me.

But not for a while.

Clerihews

In my younger days I wrote a lot of comic verse. I also developed a unique version of the clerihew that was based on the names of famous people.

Here are some of my clerihews.

Aga
Khan,
but Immanuel
Kant.

Dame May
was Witty
But John Greenleaf
was Whittier.

Oscar
was Wilde
but Thornton
was Wilder.

Clare Boothe
was Luce
but Martin
was Luther.

They are silly little efforts, but mildly amusing, I believe... perhaps because they are so economical.

4   Dona's License / Test   ⑫ DEC ⑫

SUN	MON	TUE	WED	THURS	FRI	SAT
	Prepare Driver's Test		1	2 (Moving to Orientation)	3	4 (Stuff) / Ven Werby
5	6	7 Kitchen remodel	8 Kitchen remodel	9 Kitchen remodel delayed	10 Kitchen remodel delayed	11 (Stuff) CDʳ's
12 (Wagging)	13 Kitchen remodel Tile	14 Kitchen remodel isidro	15 Kitchen remodel floor	16	17 (Kitchen remodel)	18 (Stuff) (Lewis)
19 (Gabriel + al)	20	21 (Solstice) WINTER SOLSTICE	22 (LA For)	23 SAT = 8 (LA)	24 (LA)	25 (LA) XMAS
26 (LA)	27 (LA)	28	29	30	31	

2011   ① JAN ①   2011

SUN	MON	TUE	WED	THURS	FRI	SAT
(Dr. Baker appt)						1
2 (Dona's Cert Test)	3 A = 78	4	5	6 (Dona Swim)	7 (Ang For) (Stuff)	8
9	10	11	12	13 passion cosecha	14	15 (Stuff) 12:00 AM
16	17	18	19	20	21	22 (Stuff)
23 (Gabriel)	24	25 (Gabriel Operation) INSPECTION	26 (People)	27 Judith Dermatology	28	29 (Chomsky Franklin Quandgo)
30 (Stuff)	31					

Driving License / Test in Dec. ①
Dr. Baker Dermatology in Feb. ①

Complaints:
Eight Statements About My Life
A Hyper-Reductionist View

Reviewing journal number 88, I realize that it, and probably all of the others, have a number of complaints that I seem to have been making, in countless variations, for almost fifty years.

One. *I've got a cold or a virus*...or had one or am about to get one, and I don't have any energy.

Two. *I've one, two, or three books* in various states of acceptance, rejection, production...or conception. I'm fed up with all the aggravation involved in publishing books.

Three. *I've taken a trip or am planning a trip*...or am recovering from getting a cold or something else unpleasant on a trip I've taken...

Four. *I don't have any ideas for new books*...I think I've written my last book, have reached a dead end, etc.

Five. *I'm having some problem with my computer.* Word isn't working or I've lost ten hours' worth of work...or I can't find an important file.

Six. *I'm not sleeping well*...got up very early today, was up in the middle of the night with a stuffed nose, I'm tired...and need to take a nap. Or, on rare occasions, somehow I had a wonderful night's sleep.

Seven. *The weather is lousy*...dreary, cold...it's raining or foggy out...I've been cold for 45 years here in San Francisco. Or it's a beautiful day.

Eight *Nobody appreciates me now*, though when I had my dog Patches, she did...and those who do, don't appreciate me as much as they should...and those who don't appreciate me at all are malicious beasts.

Thoreau tells a story about a publisher of his who gave him 3,000 copies of a book of his that hadn't sold. Thoreau later told a friend, "*I have a library of 5,000 books, 3,000 of which I wrote.*" In this respect, I should point out that in addition to my 94 journals, which average more than 200 pages in length, I've

PROJECTS

Over middle stall	✓	Fix Retaining / Fix carport	✓ ✓	MYTH BOOK ?		if ___ ? or the toilet	✓
Medicine ordered	✓	Silverware / Tent 8/8 °		change FONT in Gmail	✓	Fix Shed	
Fix Fence	✓	ultresound	✓	order LORAZIPAM	✓	Thompson's window fixed	✓
Screens for Bathroom windows		Repaid ? Pockets	✓			Wood for Car port replaced	
Frame panels (quit work)	✓	NEW LAPTOP ?	☒				
JOURNALS to a culling ?		Thai Trans Trip	✓				
Cough syrup Steam / Suntan lotion	✓ ✓	ULTRASOUND Scheduled	✓				
Letter for Professor	✓	Micro fiber Pillowcases	✓				
Tea cups + saucers set of four	✗	NEW POT	✓				
LAB JOB	✓	NETBOOK ?					
styles for Tablet	✓						

BOOKS BY AAB

TITLE	NO	PUBLISHER	EDITOR	
Bali Tourism ?	67	Routledge august 30	Emma Stewart	✗
Asian Icons	65	Left Coast	Mitch Allen	✓
Girl As They Said	66	Left Coast Publishers	Soogak	✓
Mythos Malin ?	68	Oakland ?		✗
Global Icons	69	Left Coast ?	Mitch Allen ?	

TRAVEL

PLACE	FROM	TO	MISC.	
RUSSIA	4/22/11	5/18/11	20 day cruise + 3 days Moscow	✓
Thailand / Laos / Cambodia	Nov. 28	Dec. 22	Pleasure + lecture	✓
SICILY ?	May 2± 2012	May 23± 2012	Pleasure	
Buenos Aires	Aug. 28 2012	Sept. 27 2012	Fulbright Senior Specialist	

Jan 29 Maggnes
Feb 5 McParlin
Feb 12 Bastille

April 27/28 Bat Mitzvah

published more than 70 books, so I can say that *I have written around 160 books, 94 of which are about myself.* Some might say all of them are about myself.

This is the ultra-short picture of my life, repeated over and over again in my journals. In between my litany of minor complaints I have speculations on all kinds of subjects and pages full of notes, charts and diagrams that I used to write my books.

My late friend Stanley Milgram, a brilliant social psychologist whom I befriended when I lived in Paris, said I was an "unclassifiable image." Irving Louis Horowitz called me an "adolescent." You can decide for yourself.

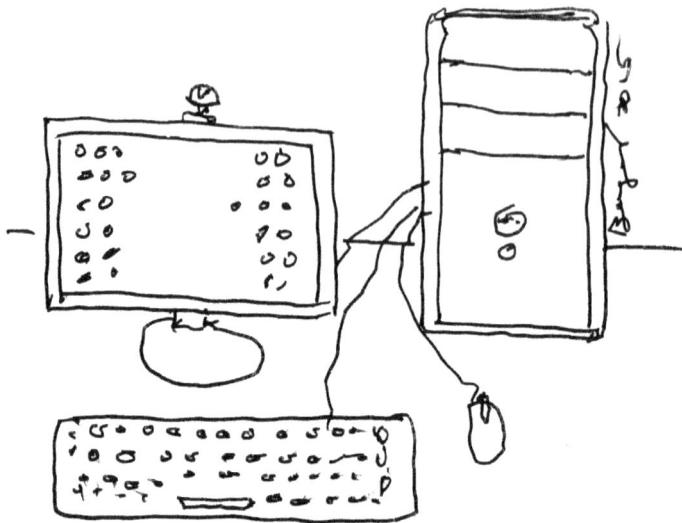

Computers and My Career as a Writer

The computer really changed my life—and, no doubt, the lives of most other writers. For what word processing did was make it possible for me to write something and then, without having to retype it, save it and revise it as many times as I felt necessary. I was liberated from Wite-Out™ and the typewriter. In addition, e-mail makes it possible for me to communicate with editors all over the world and send them material that arrives in little more than an instant.

For example, I often did book reviews for *The Journal of Communication*, a scholarly journal read by professors who teach communication in universities. The book review editor sends me e-mail messages asking me whether I'm interested in writing a review of this book or that one, and if I say "yes," she sends the book to me. When I've written the review, I e-mail it to her. Just recently, a professor in Russia sent me a book by e-mail. She divided the book into several parts and sent each part to me.

A number of years ago I thought it would be a good idea to write a dictionary in which I explained, in rather simple language, the terms used by literary theorists and culture critics. So I made a list of the most important terms and wrote my dictionary. I found that no publishers were interested, because dictionaries are seen as reference books and editors expect rather long manuscripts. So one day I sat down at the computer and pulled up the table of contents I had made for my dictionary. After studying it a while, I figured out that I could pull the various items together in chapters dealing with semiotics, psychoanalytic theory, sociological theory, Marxist theory, and literary theory. It only took a few hours to reassemble the book. Then I spent some time adding material here and there to provide continuity. It only took a couple of weeks. I now had a manuscript I titled *Cultural Criticism*, and I was able to find a publisher for it— Sage Publications, which has published something like ten of my books over the last twenty years.

So, the computer has really revolutionized my life. I know very little about computers and how they work. This always mystifies my son, Gabriel. He wants to explain to me in detail how they work, but I always say, "Look, Gabriel. If anything goes wrong, I've got you to fix things." The number of writers and others who rely on their sons and daughters—and in some cases grandchildren— to fix things when computers go awry, must be legion.

I never spend more than a couple of hours writing at a time. Because of my productivity, many of my colleagues think I'm at the computer ten or twelve hours a day, but that isn't true. When I decide to write a book, I work on it steadily, but seldom more than two or three hours at a time. You can do a lot of writing in two hours if you don't waste time daydreaming and playing computer games.

SEMIOTICS & CONSUMER CULTURE

Chapter 1 1-30 Semiotics	Chapter 2 31-54 Consumer Cultures	Ch.4 Brands of Identity 75-124	Ch.5 The Objects of our Affection 125-185
The Semiotic Theory of Saussure & Peirce: an overview	Defining Consumer Cultures	Fashion and Identity	Coffee
Some Contemporary Semiotic Theory	The Sacred origins of Consumer Cultures	Semiotics and Brands	The Toaster
Symbols	Psychological Irrationality in Consumer Cultures	Style, Choices and Identity	Swaddling Clothes
Denotation and Connotation		Hats	The "Evangel" Hamburger
Metaphor and Metonymy	Economic Theory and Consumer Cultures	Hair · Fetisher, myths and Hair · A Semiotic approach to Hair Styles in The Fighters	French Fried Potatoes
Language and Speech	Jean Baudrillard on Advertising and Consumer Cultures	Blondes: The Importance of Hair color	Fountain Pens and Ink
Codes		DESIGNER EYEGLASSES and SUNGLASSES	Bikinis
Acura: An example of Applied Semiotic analysis	Ch.3 Marketing Theory and Semiotics 55-74	TEETH	Vodka
No Signs & Signs	Ernest Dichter and Motivation Research	Wrist Watches	Beer
Signs Within Signs	Mary Douglas and Grid-Group Theory	Facial Hair in Men	Veils
Signs that Lie	News Trobyatt Advertisers	Fragrances · Brand Narcissism and L'Oreal Programs	Cornflakes
ILLUSTRATIONS	Clinton Explains that "birds of a feather flock together.."	Neckties	White Bread
Iceberg drawing	Complicating for marketers	Shoes	Bagels
Pastiche	Semiotics and Marketing Theory	Handbags and Messenger Bags	Myst
Roland Barthes		Brand Extension and Lifestyle Signifiers	Furniture
Karl Marx		Style and the Postmodern Sensibility	Teddy Bears
Sigmund Freud			Soap Powder and Detergents
Saussure			Vacuum Cleaners
C.S. Peirce			Computers
Signifier/Signified			Ch.6 186-193
Foucault Morrison			Ch.7 CODA 194-204

40

Creativity

There's comfort in creativity. We tend to regard people who are "creative" as possessing some kind of a magic gift from the gods that few people have. I don't agree. I see creativity in many places, in the doings of carpenters and cooks and lots of other people. In my career as a writer, I kept journals for many years. In those journals I often worked out, in an outline at least, what I would do when I wrote books on topics that interested me. But between the outline and the book, I often discovered that when I started writing, ideas I didn't know I had popped into my head. So, as far as I'm concerned, one aspect of creativity involves keeping journals in which I could play with ideas.

I already wrote about the page in my journal in which an image popped into my head of a man slumped over a table who had been killed four different ways. That page marked the beginning of my mystery *Postmortem for a Postmodernist*. Mitch Allen, who was then my editor at Altamira Press, originally asked me to do a comic book on Postmodernism, but I found the comic book format difficult to work with. So I decided to write a mystery with many comic book frames in it.

When I got the idea of writing a book on semiotics and consumer culture, I started playing around with ideas in my journal and drew four columns on a page of my journal that I used to think about what might be in the book. I decided to write the first chapter on semiotics, the second on consumer culture and then I did some speculating about what other topics I might include in the book.

I thought we might call it *Semiotics and Consumer Culture: An Introduction to Material Culture* by my editor at Palgrave Macmillan didn't like that title so I thought of another one, The Objects of Our Affection which was changed to *The Objects of Affection*. It was published in a series of books about semiotics and popular culture, edited by Marcel Danesi.

My list of possible topics to write about was all over the place—veils, cornflakes, toast, swaddling clothes, soap powder, vacuum cleaners, bagels, teddy bears, and so on. When I thought about the book, I concluded it would benefit from a chapter on semiotics and marketing theory and the ideas of Ernest Dichter, the "father" of motivation research, Mary Douglas and grid-group theory and various other thinkers.

In the second part of the book I decided to write about brands and the role they play in our lives and in the objects we choose to buy. I decided to use short passages of no more than 300 words, written by various scholars, to which I added comments, in the fifth chapter of the book, *The Objects of Our Affection*, and then I added some learning games and a Coda on the source (Puritanism) of our passion to consume.

I should add that here in there in my journal I devoted some space to other aspects of the book.

Below I show a somewhat different kind of page that I used to plan another book on material culture. It has four columns but I used the space in the columns to brainstorm on what I'd write about certain objects that interested me. What the journals don't reflect is the spark that happens when I start writing and ideas and insights that were somehow buried in my unconscious come to light. That's the fun part.

FREDRIC JAMESON

I also am fortunate that most of my publishers allow me to use a large number of my drawings and other images in my books. I had done drawings of Freud and Marx and Barthes and a few other important thinkers. I became interested in making other drawings and started doing cultural theorists like Fredric Jameson, Juri Lotman, Michel Foucault and Jacques Derrida.

Sometimes I devote two pages to my brainstorming efforts. What follows is work I did for a new edition of a book I wrote on visual communication, *Seeing is Believing*. In this book I could use as many images as I wanted. That's to be expected in a book on visual communication.

The first time I did the book, with a company called Mayfield, I was relatively innocent and naïve. Mayfield sent an art director to my house, who showed me many photographs and asked which ones I liked. That took about an hour. I didn't think about asking what they cost and discovered that I had spent

$4000 during that hour. That's because photographs by name photographers cost a lot of money. When the second edition came along, I took over the role of art director and managed to bring the price down to several hundred dollars.

You can see in the journal pages that I had a number of things to deal with: what topics I should add to the book, what I should write about the topics I decided to use, where I might get images I wanted and that kind of thing. When you write a book with lots of images, you have to find them, decide where to use them, think about how large or small they should be and write captions for them. It is a lot of work.

When you write a fourth edition of a book, you have to find new topics to discuss and ways to enhance previous discussions. If a book has 100,000 words, you have to add around twenty thousand words to the book and delete some material as well. In the course of my career, I've published five editions of *Media Analysis Techniques*, five editions of *Ads, Fads and Consumer Culture*, four editions of *Seeing is Believing*, and two editions of *Signs in Contemporary Culture: An Introduction to Semiotics* and two editions of *What Objects Mean: An Introduction to Material Culture*. That means I've spent years rewriting my books and searching for new material to add to them and, more painful, looking for material to delete from them.

Since I've written 70 books and eighteen new editions, you can say that I've published 88 books. But even though I've spent many years rewriting and revising my books, I've also found time to write some new ones. It seems the more I write, the more ideas I get for new projects. While I was waiting for copy-edited versions of several of my books that were in production at the same time, I found time to start a short book on the electronic devices that play such an important role in our lives.

Data-Free—or The Man
Without Quantities

There are, psychologists tell us, people who have multiple identities or multiple personalities. I have an analogous "problem," though problem probably isn't the right word: I tend to see things, not "from both sides now," as the song goes, but sometimes from five or ten different "sides" or points of view or disciplinary perspectives. I suggest that doing this, using a multi-disciplinary perspective, often offers us better ways of making sense of phenomena such as television commercials, common objects, fashions, and humor than a single or unitary perspective does. I blame this all on having seen Rashomon in 1952 at Smith College.

In a sense, when I find something I wish to analyze, I say to myself "round up the usual disciplines" and begin, often using a number of different perspectives which I believe complement one another. These disciplines are: Semiotics, which deals with signs and how we find meaning in phenomena such as films, songs, fashions, and so on; *Aesthetic Theory*, which deals with how lighting, color, cutting, sound, music, camera shots and so on generate feelings and emotions in audiences; *Psychoanalytic Theory*, which deals with unconscious elements in our thinking and acting; *Sociological Theory*, which deals with institutions and groups and matters such as race, gender, religion and class; *Political Theory*, which concerns itself with power, control and resistance in groups and society; *Anthropological Theory*, which focuses upon culture and the enculturation process; *Literary Theory*, which investigates how works of art (of all kinds) generate their effects, the various artistic devices creative artists use, and the role "readers" play; *Philosophical Thought*, which concerns itself with how we know about the world, the status of knowledge, ethical matters and related considerations; Historical Perspectives, which studies change over time...how phenomena evolve and affect/reflect the social order; and *Comparative Perspectives*, which deals with how a given text (such as *Dallas*) or other phenomena is perceived and the role it plays in different societies and cultures.

These methods are at the heart of a new subject area or "meta-discipline" (some people say I never met a discipline I

44

didn't like, but it's not true) called Cultural Studies, which, as I see things, grew out of an old one— popular culture. I made a list similar to this thirty years ago in an article titled "The Secret Agent" that I published in *The Journal of Communication*; little did I know that I was to spend the next thirty years using the various methodologies to analyze everything from television shows to hamburgers.

Cultural Studies eliminates the boundaries between elite arts and popular arts, but what it represents, I would suggest, is really a formalization (and perhaps an elaboration) of what people who had been studying popular culture were already doing (or should have been doing). Thus, for example, in the late Sixties, I used to teach a course called "The Arts, Popular Culture and Society."

Let me offer some of my crazier and more far-fetched ideas in this discussion which I call *"How I Became a Man Without Quantities."*

There was a depression over the Pacific. It was traveling Eastward, through that chaotic freeway-clogged megalopolis known as Los Angeles. It was 1982 and I had given a lecture at the Annenberg School of Communication at The University of Southern California (several years later I was to spend a year there as a visiting professor). I was having a chat with Peter Clarke, who was, at that time, dean of the school.

We were standing in one of the corridors of the expensive and very plush (though, in certain ways, remarkably dysfunctional) building that houses the Annenberg School when, during the course of our conversation, he said, "Arthur, did you ever think about the fact that you are data-free?"

"Data-free?" That is how I came to recognize, suddenly, in an epiphany, that I was a man without quantities. I wasn't sure about what he meant by that ad hoc remark. "Data-free?" Was it because I was too kind-hearted to reject the null hypothesis...or, as some have suggested, to reject any hypothesis?

The Evangelical Hamburger.

Was it because, as I had explained in 1964, that McDonald's was an "evangelical hamburger" that would eventually spread its golden arches all over the world, deluding people into thinking, by a process I called "hambourgeoisment," that their access to cheap ground meat meant they were middle class (that is, I argued, the dynamics of the McDonald's organization and their outlets resembled the dynamics of evangelical religions)?

Was he suggesting that I made everything up as I went along and merely threw charts and diagrams into my articles and books to trick sociologists (a matter rather easily done, so it seems)? I could not know.

Motelization Theory

Perhaps he had found fault with my theory of "Motelization," elaborated in the early Seventies. In an article on the subject I suggested that the American household was becoming like a motel, with the family unit more or less decomposing and disappearing (I'm exaggerating things a bit here, as is my nature). I argued that family members had become too absorbed in their own personal activities and had weakened, if not severed, their sense of connection, loyalty or responsibility towards others in their families. They seldom appeared except when they were hungry and, after "raiding" the refrigerator, zapped things in the microwave, gobbled their food down and went off to their adventures.

There were, I explained, some advantages to this arrangement. Children would no longer find it necessary to run away from home to take drugs and have sex, since they would now have direct access to their bedrooms (the parents, in this "mom and pop" form of family/motel, would take care of the laundry and provide food for meals. An ideal arrangement as far as disaffected children were concerned...and one that seems to be, more and more, the norm).

Muscle Cars and Deflowering and the Sexual Identity of Appliances

Perhaps Clarke found fault with my notion that television commercials showing "muscle" cars crashing through roadside signs and similar barriers represented, symbolically, the deflowering of virgins? Or my suggestion that household appliances had genders and could be classified according to their sexual identities (after all, most appliances, if you think about it, are receptacles and womb-like, reflecting what has been described as the "incorporative modality." The only significant household male electric appliances with the "penetrating modality" that I could find were electric knives, hand blenders, hedge trimmers and leaf blowers)? Tools, of course, are often hyper-phallic, but they aren't household appliances.

Infantile Starvation and the Purchase of Freezers

Speaking of appliances, I had also suggested that there might be a correlation between infantile hunger and the purchase of huge freezers, which some people fill with enormous amounts of food...even though there are supermarkets, open 24 hours, all over the place. This hunger, I deduced, was caused by parents who read books about babies being "spoiled" if they were fed off schedule (this is no longer held to be a good idea, but at one time it was thought to be proper).

So the parents, trying to do the right thing, let their babies, who might not have had a good feeding and were hungry, cry between feedings, until they pass out from starvation and exhaustion, but remembering, down deep in their psyches, what it was like to be hungry. In later years, when they could afford them, they purchased huge freezers and stuffed them with food.

Philosophical Perspectives: I Stink Therefore I Am and To Buy Is to Be Perceived

Maybe, I later speculated, Peter Clarke (like many others in academia, it turns out) didn't consider me to be a serious scholar. I had written an article about deodorants with a whimsical title, "I Stink, Therefore I Am," suggesting that our passion to remove body odor was tied, ultimately, to Puritanism, perfectionism, and a fear of death.

In the same vein, I had speculated, in a piece called "To Buy is to be Perceived" (playing upon Bishop Berkeley's famous dictum "to be is to be perceived"), that most of us lead lives not only of "quiet desperation" but also of relative anonymity and that, generally speaking, it is only when we purchase things that anyone pays much attention to us. And when they do, it is only pro forma. We get few personal letters nowadays, and need the bills in the mail to remind ourselves (prove to ourselves?) that we do, in fact, exist.

ErosGOPanalia: The Berger Hypottythesis.

Peter Clarke was interested in, among other things, political communication. It dawned on me that he might have read

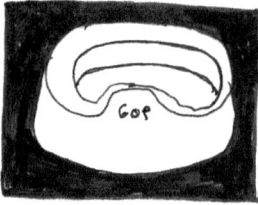

my essay about a concept I called "ErosGOPanalia," which argued that conservative Republicans like George W. Bush, members of the Grand Old Party (GOP), were anal erotics who had transferred their infantile hang-ups about retaining their stools to a fear of government spending (for anything except military weapons, that is).

It was, then, the toilet training of the young children who were to become powerful politicians, that shaped, in large measure, their political behavior as adults. The child is not only father to the psychological man, but also (and Aristotle would be pleased to hear this) to the political man. I had even written a short parody of a famous A.E. Houseman poem, to add to the argument:

> The potty does more
> Than Milton (Friedman) can
> To justify the ways of the NAM
> To man.

This concept of ErosGOPanalia was, I recognized, a radical notion. I had sent this article, subtitled "The Berger Hypottythesis," to a very distinguished economics journal and received a letter from the editor that read, in part, as follows:

> Dear Professor Berger:
>
> Thank you for sending your article, *ErosGOPanalia: The Berger Hypottythesis*, to us for consideration. The editorial staff has read your article with care and concluded, unfortunately, that it is not suitable for publication in this journal...or any that we can possibly conceive of."

Economists, of course, have no sense of humor, so I was not surprised by the rejection. I had sent my article assuming I would get a rejection something like the one I did, but the letter they sent exceeded my fondest expectations.

The TV-Guided American

I must confess: a considerable number of sociologists, anthropologists, psychologists, culture critics and others haven't liked my theories, my articles, my books and my work, in general. Some of them don't like me, either. But, I keep wondering, is it because I am a man without quantities or is it for some *other reason?*

I had written a book, *The TV-Guided American*, which was published in the mid-seventies. This book was reviewed in *The New York Times* by Jeff Greenfield with a concluding line that went something like,

Berger is to the study of television what Idi Amin is to tourism in Uganda!

Greenfield did not take kindly to my use of psychoanalytic theories and semiotics to analyze television. This is a typical layperson's response to works by scholars which is full of (to the common man and woman) "arcane" language and obscure theories.

But complicated thinking requires complicated language, even though some writers and scholars overdo things, I must admit. In the book I had contrasted football and baseball and explained that baseball was a nineteenth-century pastoral form and that it was football, with its concern with time, communication, territoriality, calculation and planning and with its spectacle, sexuality, and violence that was more reflective of contemporary American culture and society. Football, especially professional football on Sundays, I have suggested in various articles, is a functional alternative to traditional religion. The premature ending of the baseball season in 1994 showed us that we can live without baseball. But could we live without football?

White (Balloon) Bread and Lack of Ideology in America

I had also hypothesized, in an article in Rolling Stone, that traditional white or "American" balloon bread reflected our lack of ideology in America, where political parties often compromise on important issues. There was a curious correspondence, I continued, between countries that liked bread with hard crusts (such as French bread) and ideological thinking.

Our American balloon bread, which has a very soft crust, can be squeezed into a small ball and manipulated into any shape desired. Just like many of our politicians. The fact that nowadays there is a revolution in American bread and we are getting hard crusted breads in many American bakeries and stores reflects, I suggest, the fact that our politics is also getting more ideological. The amazing popularity of bagels is something I believe that political scientists should pay a good deal of attention to.

The Significant "He" and Women's Identities

Maybe Clarke found fault with my analysis of the importance of language in shaping people's consciousness. I had found a flyer, a number of years ago, at San Francisco State University announcing a meeting for feminists, saying they hoped to be "e-man-cipated." This led me to thinking about the curious fact that words indicating masculine identity are part of so many of the words dealing with women such as women, she, her, female, menstruate and menopause.

Was there, I asked, a significant "he" that was shaping women's consciousness in America and other English speaking countries? If so, changes should be made. Why Hebrew and not Shebrew? Why hedonist and not shedonist? Why heinous and not sheinous? Why heresy and not sheresy (the science that explained the power of language to shape consciousness is, of course, se-man-tics)?

Humor and Criminality: A Modest Proposal That Never Got Made

Perhaps, as I think about things, it was my work on humor and criminality that convinced Clarke that I was data-free. I had written an article about jokes Italian-Americans tell about themselves that appeared in the *San Francisco Chronicle*. These jokes were given to me by my baby-sitter, an Italian American girl. Some of these jokes follow. "How do you tell the bride at an Italian-American wedding?" *She's the one with the braided armpits.* "Why do Italian-Americans wear pointy shoes?" *So they can kill roaches when they retreat into corners.* "What's the smallest book in the library?" *Italian war heroes.* "Why don't Italians kill flies?" *It's their national bird.* " What's red, orange, yellow, green, blue and purple?" *An Italian, dressed up.*

A short while after this article was published I received a letter from Leslie Wilkins, at the time a professor of criminology at The University of California at Berkeley. He was interested in investigating whether criminals have a different sense of humor from non-criminals. We applied for a grant of $500,000 with him as principal investigator to test this hypothesis but, tragically, were turned down. It was, he said, the only grant proposal he had ever made that was rejected.

Wilkins wanted to find out whether criminals had a different sense of humor from non-criminals to further knowledge, for essentially intellectual reasons, one might say (I had thought it would be good to do a multi-cultural study, testing criminals not only in America, in New York, San Francisco, New Orleans, and Miami Beach, but also in Paris, Rome, London [during the theatre season, of course], the Riviera, Rio, Hong Kong, Ko Samui and Bali). But I had—though I never told him so—other notions, involving the criminal sense of humor and public policy.

I had a modest proposal to make, that, alas, never got made.

I reasoned as follows: if we discover that criminals do, in fact, have a different sense of humor than non-criminals, we can develop a humor test, an instrument, which would allow us to identify or discover not only who are and who are not criminals, but also, more importantly, who will be criminals.

We could give this test to children and adolescents and if they showed criminality in their sense of humor, I reasoned, we could throw them in jail *before* they committed their crimes. This would save people, I suggested, from the terrible feelings of anguish and violation they suffer when mugged or robbed and from the loss of money and property from burglaries and other crimes.

The Berger-Wilkins Criminal Sense of Humor Instrument would also save the taxpayers a considerable amount of money wasted, generally, on programs by psychologists and social-workers for disturbed and criminal youth. When, if ever, problem youth or career criminals tested negatively on the criminal sense of humor test, we could let them go, with little fear of recidivism.

The Man Without Quantities Considers Data

There are, I concluded, two ways of looking at the notion of being "data-free" (a wit—I believe it was Robert Benchley—said "The world is divided into two groups of people. Those who divide the world into two groups of people and those who don't"). The first is that one has no factual information or content and the second is that one does not use statistics and quantitative data. Which was I? Or was it both?

Ironically, my first published paper, on weekly magazines in Italy, was full of numerical data. I had made content analyses of a number of Italian magazines, such as *Oggi, Europeo,* and *Epoca,* and had a good deal of quantitative material in it. This article was published in an excellent Italian sociological journal, Il Mulino. I had suggested, in the conclusion of the article, that Italian weeklies were like dinosaurs—with gigantic bodies (circulations) and tiny brains (editorial staffs). After that article I more or less abandoned quantitative research, though I often cite data from other researchers in my articles and books.

Unrecognized Resemblances and Hidden Meanings

What Clarke was probably referring to was my use of analogies and metaphors in my work. If I argue that neon cocktail signs which show swizzle sticks pointing at cherries in cocktail glasses are phallic, I am suggesting, really, that there is an analogy that can be drawn (and is drawn, literally, by the neon sign makers) between the signs with their swizzle sticks and a man's penis and a woman's genitals. Whether people who make the signs or those who see the signs recognize this is not terribly relevant. The term cocktail is another give away, since "cock" refers to a man's penis and women are, in slang, often called "pieces of tail."

People, I believe, are seldom aware of the deeper meanings and hidden aspects of their activities. People do things, for a variety of reasons, many of which are unconscious, and social scientists and researchers (as well as therapists) try to figure out: 1. What people actually do, in contrast to what they say they do or think they do; and 2.Why they do what they do or did what they did. We often find ourselves trying to find out about the unknown on the basis of the known. Thus, when I argued that most household appliances were feminine, I suggested that, in certain respects, they were "womb-like" and that this had interesting implications.

The Man Without Quantities Discusses Knowing X in Terms of Y

This matter of finding out about unknown things in terms of known things, of seeing things in terms of other things, can be labeled, at the highest level of generality (which is where men without quantities like to dwell), as knowing X in terms of Y.

Metaphor is, in essence, making sense of one thing in terms

of another. We all tend to see things in terms of other things all the time, but we never pay any attention to this matter. My point is, then, that seeing similarities and making associations between and among phenomena where we hadn't seen them or recognized them is nothing new. The question is whether the similarities perceived are actually there (and not just in our imaginations) and, if so, what significance they have. It becomes a matter of interpretation. But even if I were a man with quantities, and data rich instead of data free, I would still have to interpret my numerical data.

In this respect, consider the science of Economics, probably the most scientific of the social scientists. Economists, using the same data—statistics from various governmental agencies, for example— often disagree about what they mean. So you can't escape from some kind of an interpretation and "going beyond" one's data. And that's assuming that the data are accurate and correct.

Data Man Versus Data-Free Man

Let us assume, using the perspective found in comic books, that we have two heroes who are researchers—Data Man and Data-Free Man. There are considerable differences in the way our two heroes see and make sense of the world, which I will explain below. DATA MAN wants information, the Mean, his N strives to reach infinity, is quantitative, stresses ingenuity in design, loves statistics and likes quantifiable subjects. He obtains certainty at the price of triviality. He wants to count every grain of sand in the universe. DATA-FREE MAN stresses interpretation, meaning, his N is 1, is qualitative, shows ingenuity in analysis, focuses on texts rather than audiences, uses concepts from various domains, seeks subjects useful for theorizing, and achieves significance at the price of uncertainty. He sees the universe in a grain of sand.

This oppositions oversimplifies things, of course, but it does show how different the orientation of quantitative and qualitative scholars can be.

Quantitative researchers often use sophisticated statistical methods but, because they are forced to, frequently deal with relatively trivial matters–ones that lend themselves to quantification. Qualitative researchers, at the other extreme, often deal with important social, political, and economic matters, and use concepts and theories from psychoanalytic thought,

Marxist thought, semiotic thought, and the likes–which often yield interesting ideas but do not give certainty.

For Data Man, designing research so one gets good data (and not the wrong data) is very difficult. For Data-Free Man, applying the right concepts correctly and "not going off the deep end" is the problem. The optimal situation is to figure out how to use statistics and quantitative data and combine this material with qualitative and theoretical material. The best scholars do this, I would suggest, or occupy some middle ground between the two extremes that I've sketched out. But it isn't easy being both Data Man and Data-Free Man at the same time.

Conclusions of a Man Without Quantities, a Practicing Theoretician

I am, as I have explained, a Man Without Quantities, and because I am "data-free" and have no statistics to "massage," I cannot, so the logic of the men with quantities suggests, do research. When I told a colleague of mine that I had written a book on research (one that, incidentally, has gone through a number of printings) he laughed and said "What do you know about research, Arthur? You make it all up as you go along" (I had been rash enough to joke, in one of my books, that I don't do research and make everything up as I go along and put charts in to fool sociologists)!

Since I've published more than 130 articles and more than seventy books, if I don't do research I must, at the very least, have a really fantastic imagination. Maybe being data-free is actually a kind of postmodernist stance? Maybe qualitative scholars like myself should best be seen as fiction writers? Fiction writers use fiction to convey truths about people–and isn't truth what we're after?

Might Peter Clarke have been right? Might I be data-free, a Man Without Quantities? But I like to think that I, and other qualitative researchers (if that phrase is not an oxymoron) have qualities–imaginative, literary, artistic, ethical, and otherwise, and that they count for something.

Decoder-Man

In the Spring 1974 issue of *The Journal of Communication*, I published an article titled "The Secret Agent," and then took on, for the fun of it, the mock-identity of being a scholar and secret agent. I used a caricature I had made of myself as a secret agent in letters and I also made an embosser with my name and writer, artist, and secret agent on it. I often stamped my letters with this embosser.

But after a number of years, as I wrote more and more from

the standpoint of a semiotician, I decided to add another superhero characterization to my repertoire, and so I became "Decoder-Man." I did a caricature of myself as a super-hero called "Decoder-Man," whose mission it is (comic strip heroes always have missions) to decode anything and everything that strikes my attention as being interesting.

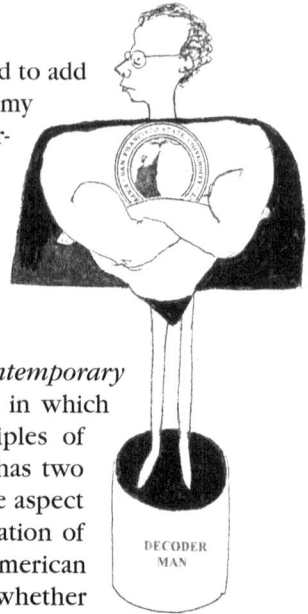

I wrote a small book, *Signs in Contemporary Culture: An Introduction to Semiotics*, in which I explained some of the basic principles of semiotics. In this book, each chapter has two parts: part one is an explanation of some aspect of semiotics, and part two is an application of this topic to some kind of signifier in American culture. My thesis was that we are all, whether we recognize it or not, semioticians. That is, we all try to make sense of matters like facial expressions, clothes people wear, people's body language, status symbols, and so on.

The important thing is to see such phenomena as signs, and more specifically signifiers, and to try and figure out what the signifieds are. What semiotics does, among other things, is to attempt to understand how people decode things and to formulate rules for doing so and offer explanations of how this decoding should be done.

My book *Bloom's Morning* analyzes American culture by decoding the various rituals and objects that are part of a typical male American's morning. I did this because I see American culture (and all cultures) as full of signs. Charles Sanders Peirce, one of the founding fathers of semiotics, explained it this way. He writes that "...the universe if perfused with signs, it is not composed exclusively of signs." When you see things not in terms of being objects or in terms of their function but as signs, you are then seeing the world from a semiotic point of view. And if everything is a sign—granted that some signs are more important than others—there's plenty of work for me, as Decoder-Man, and for other decoder men and women, to do.

Freudian Slips

I often use Freud's concepts in my work, because I find them so useful. They help me explain the significance of events in narratives that often seem trivial or meaningless. Freud's notion that seemingly unimportant slips of the tongue often reveal important things about a person is the metaphor I use in a good deal of my work. If you don't believe in the unconscious, of course, then life becomes much simpler when you interpret a text. You take everything a person says or does as not having any deeper meaning or hidden significance, and that's that.

I wouldn't say that I'm a doctrinaire Freudian and accept everything he's written as the gospel, but I don't see how you can analyze media and popular culture without recognizing the importance of the unconscious and of the various defense mechanisms Freud discusses and other similar matters that fall under the rubric of psychoanalytic thought.

In 1984 I wrote an article for the *Los Angeles Times* in which I suggested that video games were masturbatory activities (kids loved to play with their joy-sticks) and that Pac-Man was, from a developmental point of view, a regressive game. We had been playing phallic games like Space Invaders in which we shot down aliens with cannons and ray guns, and then, with Pac-Man, we regressed to the oral stage—eating dots.

The newspaper received a number of letters from outraged readers who though my article was sheer lunacy and said so in very forceful ways. The nice thing about Freudian theory is that we can explain this reaction as a kind of repression on the part of the people who could not face up to the sexual nature of this video game.

I explained once that the Washington Monument was a gigantic phallic symbol—a suitable monument for the father of our country. This was greeted by many with disdain. Interestingly enough, a sign maker who did many of the signs in Las Vegas once revealed that the owners of the hotels told him they wanted "a big phallic symbol going up in the sky as far as you can make it." I had analyzed household appliances in terms of whether they were masculine (penetrating) or feminine (incorporating) and psychoanalyzed Dick Tracy as an obsessive with a distorted superego.

I developed a game I played in my criticism class in which we analyzed American culture in terms of Freud's Id, Ego and Superego concepts (cities, areas of the country, television programs, among other things) and I had some fun with an article that was a put-on—in which I suggested that Republicans in Congress, who didn't want to spend money for education, social welfare and so on, were anal-erotics.

Fry, the Chimp Tickler

If you are someone named Berger, it is a wonderful thing to have a friend whose last name is Fry. I always think it would be great to do a book with him, so people could talk about "Berger and Fry's book...." I once edited a book of my articles that I called *The Evangelical Hamburger*. How marvelous it would be if we did a second edition, with some of his articles in it, so people could talk about "Berger and Fry's *Evangelical Hamburger*." An even better idea would for us to do a vegetarian cookbook— Berger and Fry's *Vegetarian Cookbook*. That is close to being a paradox, a concept very dear to good Dr. Fry.

William Fry is a psychiatrist, a notorious chimp tickler, who was associated with Stanford University for many years, before he retired. While there he worked on a project with Gregory Bateson involving humor and this experience led Bill to write a very important book about humor, *Sweet Madness*. We share an interest in humor. He now lives in Nevada City, California— in the "Gold Country," so we don't get to see one another very often, alas. Nevada City is about a three-and-a-half hour drive from Mill Valley, where I live.

Before he left the Bay Area, Bill and I organized a humor society which I called BAHA "The Bay Area Humor Association." Generally speaking, since San Francisco State was the most convenient place for professors and students from Stanford and Berkeley and other schools to get together, we held our meetings there. We met every two or three months for a couple of years or so. At each meeting, someone would give a presentation.

Once I got a professional joke writer named John Cantu to give a workshop on writing jokes. He used to sell his material to disc jockeys. Cantu showed the professors how he could take a subject, brainstorm on different aspects of it, and then crank out forty or fifty gags, wisecracks, and one-liners, in a very mechanical manner. It blew everyone's mind. Many of the gags he produced weren't funny at all. "These jokes may not all be funny," he said, "but they're all *valid*." Many years later I invited John to give a talk at a class I taught on comedy. He gave an hour disquisition on what to do with the microphone if you do stand-up comedy. It was absolutely fabulous and showed how complicated that matter of performing comedy is.

When Bill is in the San Francisco area, we often get together for lunch; often at Dim Sum restaurants. It's always quite comic, because Bill is the supreme slow eater of the Western United States (and perhaps the whole country). You have to be very alert and slow down your eating to a snail's pace to match him. It could easily take him five minutes to eat four little shrimp balls. He also tends to swish tea around in his mouth, so drinking tea with him becomes a minor ordeal...though you can fill your cup up four or five times while you're waiting for Bill to swallow a mouthful of tea.

And when we meet we plan various projects and schemes involving, generally speaking, getting grants so we can go to nice places like Spain and investigate Spanish humor...and so on. We once submitted a grant application to some government agency to investigate Spanish humor, even though neither of us spoke Spanish. It was rejected by the committee that evaluated grant applications 11 to 0. The members of the committee must have a good laugh when they read our grant application. So all was not lost, since Bill and I both believe in the supreme importance of laughter.

Humor

I see myself as essentially a humorist (more on this shortly) who did his gigs in universities, not comedy clubs. This has caused some problems for me with some academicians and some students, who take themselves seriously. Most of the scholars I have met who are outstanding in one way or another have a very good sense of humor. People who have confidence in themselves can enjoy the comedy of life; for example, my friend Aaron Wildavsky, who was a world-class political scientist, had a wonderful sense of humor. The first time we met he told me some wonderful Jewish jokes. We even talked about collaborating on a book on humor before his untimely death and we did work on an article together that was published in *Society* magazine.

The distinguished philosopher Gustav Bergman, with whom I studied at the University of Iowa, once said "If I had the choice between making a very funny joke which would cost me the friendship of my best friend and not telling the joke, I would tell the joke." That statement liberated me and I spent the rest of the semester making puns and other comic statements in the poor man's course.

I don't tell jokes, as a rule. I once wrote something titled "how to be funny without telling jokes for people who tell jokes without being funny." What I do is play with ideas, play with sounds, make puns and sometimes witticisms, and generally clown around—too much for my own good at times, I fear. I come from a family of humorists. My mother told dirty jokes on her death bed. My father used to tell me stories about the "no-soapie Indians" and liked to draw cartoons. My brother is a compulsive punster and after a while becomes absolutely obnoxious and impossible to be with, since he is incapable of not punning. He puns in three languages and finds a way to make a pun on the average of once or twice a minute, or so it seems. There probably is a disease for that affliction, but I don't know the name for it.

And I draw funny illustrations for my books (and books by others, at times) and write articles in which I play with ideas and make wild analogies. This doesn't mean that I'm not serious at times, but generally speaking, I see the absurdity in life and in the best postmodern tradition, I am, at times, a sociological "put-on" artist and ironist. Some of my students have told me I'm "far out," but I explain to them that, in truth, I'm close to the center of contemporary intellectual thought, and that they are "far in." There's nothing students dislike more than being told they're "far in" or that they are "boring." They seem to think only they have the right to use that word to dismiss everything that they don't find entertaining.

One of the secrets of being a humorist is to do comic things but with a straight face, and to offer comic ideas in the guise of solemn social science. I wrote essays in which I considered the sexual identity of household appliances—those with the incorporative modality were obviously feminine (that's most of our appliances) and those with the penetrating modality were masculine (the electronic knife and little else). In short I was having fun with my analyses which often seemed absurd to many social scientists and others. They were absurd, and yet, I would argue, they had an element of truth to them.

I also did some scholarly work on humor and made a content analysis of all the works of humor I had in my house—this includes comic books, joke books, short stories, novels, books of humorous verse, and plays. From this material I isolated what I call the 45 techniques of humor...such as insult, exaggeration, bombast, and facetiousness. These techniques, I argue—and demonstrated in my book, *The Art of Comedy Writing*, have been used by comedy playwrights from the Roman times to the present and are the building blocks of comedy. Any example of humor, in any genre, from any time period and in any culture, I suggest, makes use of one or more of these techniques.

These 45 Techniques of Humor fall into four categories: humor of *language*, humor involving *logic*, humor dealing with *identity*, and what I call *action* humor (though visual humor might be a more accurate term). I have charts in which I've numbered each of these techniques and one of the exercises I use in teaching comedy writing is to give my students the charts and a list of jokes and ask them to list the techniques found in each joke. They come up with a "formula" for each joke or other comic text.

45 Techniques of Humor

LANGUAGE	LOGIC	IDENTITY	ACTION
Allusion	Absurdity	Before/After	Chase
Bombast	Accident	Burlesque	Slapstick
Definition	Analogy	Caricature	Speed
Exaggeration	Catalogue	Eccentricity	
Facetiousness	Coincidence	Embarrassment	
Insults	Comparison	Exposure	
Infantilism	Disappointment	Grotesque	
Irony	Ignorance	Imitation	
Misunderstanding	Mistakes	Impersonation	
Over-literalness	Repetition	Mimicry	
Puns/Wordplay	Reversal	Parody	
Repartée	Rigidity	Scale	
Ridicule	Theme & Variation	Stereotype	
Sarcasm	Unmasking		
Satire			

Techniques of Humor in Alphabetical Order

1. Absurdity
2. Accident
3. Allusion
4. Analogy
5. Before/After
6. Bombast
7. Burlesque
8. Caricature
9. Catalogue
10. Chase Scene
11. Coincidence
12. Comparison
13. Definition
14. Disappointment
15. Eccentricity
16. Embarrassment
17. Exaggeration
18. Exposure
19. Facetiousness
20. Grotesque
21. Ignorance
22. Imitation
23. Impersonation
24. Infantilism
25. Insults
26. Irony
27. Mimicry
28. Mistakes
29. Misunderstanding
30. Over-literalness
31. Parody
32. Puns
33. Repartée
34. Repetition
35. Reversal
36. Ridicule
37. Rigidity
38. Sarcasm
39. Satire
40. Scale, Size
41. Slapstick
42. Speed
43. Stereotypes
44. Theme & Variation.
45. Unmasking

A joke might use as many as three or four of these techniques. Thus, a joke that makes use of three of the techniques in it might be listed as: 25 (insults), 30 (misunderstanding) and 43 (stereotypes). This listing of techniques by their numbers brings to mind a famous joke about comedians who have gathered together for a conference. Since they know all the jokes in the world, they number them. There are two punchlines that I've seen for this set up. In the first version, a comedian gets up and yells "25,004." Nobody laughs. One comedian leans over to a friend and says "He never could tell a joke." In the second, a comedian gets up and yells "five billion, two hundred and sixty thousand, five hundred and four." At this, everyone bursts into laughter. One comedian leans over and says to a friend, "Never heard that one before."

Let me now take a joke and show the different techniques that are operating in it. This joke is called "the Tan," and is one of my favorites.

> A man goes to Miami for a vacation. After a few days there he looks in a mirror and notices he has a beautiful tan all over his body, with the exception of his penis. He decides to remedy the situation, and have a perfect tan all over his body. So the next morning he gets up early, goes to a deserted section of the beach, and starts putting sand over his body until only his penis remains exposed to the sun. A couple of little old ladies happen to walk by shortly after the man has finished shoveling the sand all over himself. One notices the penis sticking out of the sand. She points it out to her friend. "When I was twenty, I was scared to death of them. When I was forty, I couldn't get enough of them. When I was sixty, I couldn't get one to come near me…And now they're growing wild on the beach!"

What techniques can be found in this joke. One thing we find is eccentricity (15)—the man who feels he must have a tan over every inch of his body. Another technique comparisons (12). The woman talks about her relations to men, and their penises, when she was 20, 40 and 60. In addition, there is the matter of making mistakes (29), found in the punch line—the woman thinks that penises can grow wild on the beach. It might also be that there is unmasking and revelation of character (45) since the elderly lady tells us about her relations with men over her life. I think you can see from this example that jokes are often rather complicated little stories that contain a number of different techniques that generate humor. In addition to analyzing this joke in terms of the techniques of humor it uses, I've also interpreted from psychoanalytic, Marxist, semiotic, Feminist and sociological perspectives.

I am also the founder and director general for life of a very selective humor organization, California Lovers of Wit and Nonsense (CLOWN), an entity that I created and whose membership I limit to one person—myself.

I tried to found a scholarly organization, Studies in Popular Art and Media (SPAM) and wrote to the Hormel corporation to see whether they might fund it. They were not amused.

Iowa City: The Athens of the Midwest

I was originally going to get my master's degree in journalism from the University of California at Berkeley. After I graduated from the University of Massachusetts, I drove up to Alaska with a friend, looking for big bucks. But things had closed down, so I ended up getting a job in a department store that was opening up and living in a log cabin with five other men—most of whom were in construction and made huge amounts of money. When I had made enough money to get out of Fairbanks, I flew down to Berkeley and showed up at Cloyne Court, where I was given a room. I took a couple of courses that summer and was all set to stay at Berkeley when my father sent me a letter informing me that I had been granted a scholarship at the University of Iowa. So off to Iowa I went, not realizing that I had a quarter-time assistantship. At least I didn't have to pay my tuition. I found an unheated room over an all-night hamburger joint, Joe and Leo's in five corners—not far from the campus. My floor was all heterosexual; the floor below was all gay.

At the University of Iowa, one of my favorite teachers was Gustav Bergmann. He was a short, bald man who spoke with a German accent. He had been associated with the Vienna School of Logical Positivists—the school that taught everyone that a sunset was merely "shimmering photons." Bergmann was professor of psychology and philosophy at Iowa, and had the habit of walking up and down the corridors in the building where he had his office, smoking a big cigar and thinking. I took several courses with him and found him to be a remarkable teacher.

He had what might best be described as a "powerful presence," and knew it. He thought that it was the professor who was all important and that a big class with a great professor was to be preferred to a small class with an ordinary professor. "Vat vould you rather do," he would say. "Take zum class mit only ten shtudents in it mit a professor who's done nutting or take a class mit sixty shtudents in it but haf as your professor zumbody like Gustave Bergmann?" I remember what he said in class when the papers had a story about Arthur Miller marrying Marilyn Monroe and someone asked him what he thought about it. "Pree-poshterous!" I was a graduate student in the journalism department at Iowa, having gone on to Iowa after I graduated with a degree in English at the University of Massachusetts.

My professors there had dissuaded me from going for an advanced degree in English. "It's not for you," they said. "It's too specialized and rather technical. You wouldn't enjoy it." They didn't think I had the right personality for graduate work in literature—and I'm sure they were correct. So I decided to take an advanced degree in journalism and become a writer. At Iowa I was, for a while, the theater critic, the art critic and the music critic for *The Daily Iowan*—what I would describe as the "cultural commissar of Iowa City." I once interviewed Dimitri Mitroupolous who was about to conduct a concert there. He gave me a wonderful quote. "It's corn before culture in Iowa," he said.

Although I took journalism courses, in the magazine sequence (headed by William Porter, who was later to move to the University of Michigan) I also took painting courses with Jim Leshay and writing courses, in the writer's workshop. My teacher in the workshop was the fabulous Marguerite Young.

Marguerite Young was a fascinating woman who was working on a novel, later published (after nineteen years of effort, or was it only seventeen?) as *Miss MacIntosh, My Darling*. Marguerite taught a course in creative writing. Our textbooks were William James book on psychology and *The Fifty-Minute Hour.* Marguerite was probably in her early forties when I studied with her, had bangs and long hair...and had attracted a number of what we would now call "groupies" around her—including a number of rather beautiful women who were interested in writing and in being with creative people. Every once in a while she would give readings—chapters from *Miss MacIntosh*...that were absolutely marvelous.

She was very encouraging and always was talking about her literary friends in New York, a city she longed to live in. It seemed as if she knew every important woman writer in New York and mentioned them all the time. Marguerite was a great name dropper.

She eventually left Iowa and got an apartment in Greenwich Village. Marguerite's apartment in New York City had all kinds of photographs taped to the walls and ceilings and was "magical," as was Marguerite. When her book was published it got a front page review in *The New York Times Book Review* but it was 1200 pages of lyric poetry and was not a popular success. Marguerite taught by talking about how she worked, talking about other writers, talking about writing, suggesting books to read and encouraging students to write and persevere. Students would read their work in progress and we would discuss what we liked and didn't like about the works. We had a long story or part of a novel as our assignment. I wrote a story about a chameleon figure, who changed himself to be like those around him (much like Woody Allen's celebrated *Zelig*). "You've got to learn how to dramatize the inner self," she used to say. "Dramatize the inner self."

Eleven days after I got my Master's degree from the University of Iowa I was drafted and ended up being stationed in Washington, D.C. I used to go up to New York from time to time and visited her. The tragedy of her life was that she loved, hopelessly, Gustav Bergmann. I happened to be in Iowa City in 1985, attending a conference, and called Bergmann. He was suffering from Alzheimer's disease and died a short while later. The last time I spoke with Marguerite Young, in the late 1980's, she said, "I never told you this, Arthur, when you were my student, but I always loved you."

I had some good friends at Iowa, most of whom had disappeared. But I have kept in touch with several of them—Gerry Siegel, who was in speech pathology, and Floyd Horowitz, who was getting a Ph.D. in English. When I mentioned I'd met Floyd Horowitz to Bill Porter, he said "Floyd likes to do research." Floyd's wife, Fran, was teaching third grade when I left Iowa to go into the Army. She went on to get a Ph.D. and to do some important research. She is now president of the City University of New York's Graduate Center. A great deal can happen in 45 years!

Jewish Humorist

Being Jewish I am (it almost comes naturally), like many Jews, a Jewish humorist. There is an enigma about Jewish humor. How come the Jewish people, who have suffered so much, have such an incredible sense of humor? "Why do you want to know?" would be a Jewish response, since Jews are supposed to always answer questions with questions. Another answer might be, "you don't have to suffer to be a good Jewish comedian—but it really helps!"

It is my sense of humor that characterizes me and which has, to a certain extent, shaped my life and career. I am an ironist and a trickster, as I mention from time to time in the book, and I see life as comic. Maybe even absurd (one of my colleagues in a former department wrote a report, in his evaluation of me when I was being considered for promotion to full professor, "we thought he was an absurdist, but then decided he was an absurdity." I thought it was a wonderful line).

He also told me that my books were unpublishable, even though I had published half a dozen books at the time. "You trick editors into publishing your work," he said. "Your books should never have been published." When I asked him how come he had never published anything, he told me "my work is too good to be published." And that's where we left it. I have continued to trick editors and publish unpublishable books and his career can be characterized as doing scholarly work that is too good to be published. Actually, I don't think he ever did any scholarly work and I'd be surprised if he ever published anything more than perhaps a chapter from his dissertation, if that.

If you understand my orientation to the world and you realize that I don't take myself seriously (which is where some of the trouble comes) you get a different perspective on my work—or much of it, I should say—than if you don't. It was Santayana who said "the universe is an equilibrium of idiocies," and I think he was right.

A number years ago, my good friend Irving Louis Horowitz told me I was an adolescent...or maybe it was that I act like an adolescent. At the time I was 60 or so. I took that remark as a compliment. Irving is one of my favorite gullible editors that I've "fooled," in case you're interested—but only ten or eleven times.

He sits in his office in a beaten up old Army barracks on the Rutgers campus with two neurotic dogs and reads book manuscripts and writes to thousands of people, while also writing an incredible number of articles and books. Over the course of twenty years we've written quite a few letters to one another, since I also edit a series of reprints of classic books in mass communication for him.

"You're lettering me to death," he once said.

This was before E-mail, mind you. So I've let up on the letters and hardly e-mail him, either. Irving is responsible (notice I didn't say guilty, though some would say that's probably a more correct word) for my publishing three scholarly books on humor...and getting a number of other humor scholars to write for Transaction or have their books reprinted by Transaction. Fortunately, he has a great sense of humor. As he wrote, once, in rejecting one of my manuscripts—"I may be crazy, Arthur...but I'm not *that* crazy!"

After I semi-retired from San Francisco State (an utterly absurd institution), I started writing comic mysteries in which I could satirize academics, administrators, and universities. I assuage my hostility by murdering numerous professors, and teach my readers something about some subject. After I wrote *Postmortem for a Postmodernist*, about Postmodernism, I wrote *The Hamlet Case*, in which, as I mentioned earlier, a crazed professor murders the editorial board of Shakespeare Studies, which he edits. He fears the board is going to name someone else as editor, so he bumps them off—but not before each of them has offered a different interpretation of *Hamlet*.

Killing professors, even though it is only in works of fiction, is, I find, very therapeutic. In my book titled *The Mass Comm Murders*, I have five professors, all media theorists, murder one another. I hope that students who read this book will learn a good deal about media theories, while enjoying the pleasure of seeing professors, hated authority figures for many, bumped off.

I used to write a good deal of comic verse, since I like to play with words. The first week I was in Minneapolis, as a graduate student in American Studies, I went to a party full of professors from the English department. One of the professors was holding forth about how terrible some poet named John Silken was. I asked him, "are you trying to make a sow's ear out of Silken verse?" It was that question that established my reputation with the English department as something of a wit.

JOSE LUIS CAIVANO caivano@fadv. Uba.ar 4702-6009 home 4789-6289 office ciudad de la Paz 3485, BA	See 9/27 event from Joe fox msg ol e-mail	CANTINA PIERINO $ AR 40 people	Carlota Restaurant Casa Salt Shaker EL SANJUANINO LA CHOLITA
	MABEL LOPEZ YCHODOS@FADU. UBA.AR	MARA STEINER marasteiner04 @yahoo.com.AR	LAS CABRAS Star Hop in Palermo
	BEATRIZ SZNAIDER BSZNAIDER@ GMAIL.com		LA CABRERA Palermo 647 Dinner club
MARIA LEDESMA MVLEDESMA@ hotmail.com Maria del Valle. Ledesme@ quiet. com	SANDRA VALDETTARO@ GMAIL.com KEIRA MILLS Fulbright iia	La PCab Prof. Raul Mudo MEDA@UCALP. EDU.AR	EL TRAPICHE GRAN PARILLA De PLATA EL ESTABLO AQVELLOS AÑOS non use
LEONOR ARFUCH LARFUCH@FADU. UBA.AR	APARTMENT IN Bueno Aires Torres Manuel ANCHORENA No: 1159 3965- 4th floor 0211 Recoleta AGUERO	Rosare Prof Elizabeth martines ELI. MAGUIRRE @ Gmail.com	EL ESTRE BE or Posta in Recoleta LA CHOLITA Recoleta
ROSARIO		Beatris (LordLady) 4291-0508	CUMANA Rodregez Pena
LA PLATA ROSARIO Prof. Elizabeth MARTINEZ & AGUIRE UWT NO: +33257.535935 MALATOT 415 488-3285 CITIBANK Belgrano Av. Cabildo 2397	ctrd Recoleta Ayccucho 1416 Belr. Pachaco de heh A Pena street Temple Liberty Sgn. de Congr - Ixvalda Recoleta 2 A floor Cerrito 269 BEATRIZ SZNAIDER ARANGUREN 58 Sulte A Recoletoria	PAULA SIGANOVICH 3925 concepcion Arenal 4552-1094 39 Bus To: MARIA LEDESMA @yahoo.com.AR	P.gem Cafe Victoria clorits Sud shop Temple Liberty Recoleta
			PESOS DOLLARS
BELGRAU BET the Community clond Belgrano MIZRAH	MARA.STEINER04 ELIZABETH MARTINEZ de AGUIRE ELI.MAGUIRE@ GMAIL.com	1 22 10 2.20 15 3.30 20 4.40 25 5.50 30 6.60 5 1.10 2 44 3 66 4 88 6 1.33 7 154	
Rosario LA PAZ	ANCHORENA AGUERO 5185	JUGOSO PANIFICO Bakery	40 8.80 50 11.00 100 22.0

Keeping My Journals
or Are my Journals Keeping Me?

In 1955 or 1956 I started keeping a journal, and have been at it ever since. Several of my teachers at the University of Massachusetts had suggested I do so, but I didn't take them up on it. Then, one day, I happened to buy a book that I could use as a journal (it was a dummy book that I got in a sale of all the books you could carry out in your hands for $5.00 from a bookstore in Iowa City) and I started with my journal.

I've written 94 journals—most of them on blank artist's notebooks that are approximately five inches by eight inches and bound. During my year in Italy I didn't have a notebook so I got something similar at a stationery store, but it was twice as long. And I have one that is 8.5 inches by 11 inches. But most of them are five by eight.

All of my books have come out of my journals. I can see, when I look back, how an idea would come into my head; how I would play around with it; how I would list ideas I might deal with in it; and then, sometimes years later, I'd write a book on that idea or subject. In my journals I write about books I'm writing, books I've written, books I'm thinking of writing…and about every day, mundane things like how well I slept, what I had to eat for lunch, what the weather is like, and so on.

For example, in a journal I wrote starting on January 23, 1991, I have a notation on page 145: "Novel Textbook Ideas." Under this notation I write the following: "1. Explore a topic in form of a didactic novel…i.e. a textbook buried in a murder mystery. 2. Subject of Textbook? 3. (Style: a parody). 4. Critics fighting about how to interpret some text…*Hamlet*? 5. At a conference in a large mansion?"

This note was to be repeated, in varying forms, for another six years until I wrote a comic mystery novel about postmodernism, *Postmortem for a Postmodernist*, and then another one, *The Hamlet Case*, about different ways of interpreting Hamlet. In later journals I worked out exactly how I was going to write each of these books—and another one, about media theorists, *The Mass Comm Murders*. I have some pages in my journals

73

that have three or four (and occasionally more) columns in them in which I write down notes about the characters and their relationships with one another.

So I can, if I dig around enough in my journals, trace when I first got an idea for a book and then see how my ideas about the book evolved over time—in some cases a number of years—until I wrote the book. In 1996, in volume 66, I find myself working away on my *Hamlet* book. And on page 114, I have the word HAMLET in large letters near the top of the page. Under this I have two notes of interest: 1. (Turn it into a murder mystery???) 2. Use various methodologies to analyze it…in form of a murder mystery…confessions of a murderer??"

Then, under those notes, I have what turned out to be (with certain modifications made later) the first chapter in *The Hamlet Case*.

It was I who drove a knife into the breast of the psychoanalytic critic Melanie JungFreud, and I who shot that bitch, the feminist critic, Anastasia Spivak-Trotsky and I who decapitated the Marxist critic Jamison Kellner and I who poisoned the structuralist Umberto Gadda, and I who pushed the literary theorist and critic Anne-Sophie Kristela off a cliff. And I who strangled Midoro Domo, the Japanese literary theorist. My name is Agostino Glioma and I am editor of Hamlet Studies, a journal devoted to Hamlet…."

I revised this opening paragraph somewhat as I got into the book. On the next page I list the characters, who they are killed, and do some plotting.

I've been reading Shakespeare Studies.

HUNTER CHATS WITH MELANIE JUNGFREUD…

So I can say that on Monday, August 19th, 1966 I started actually writing *The Hamlet Case*, though I had been thinking about doing so for years. In the pages that come after 114, I have lists of attributes of the characters, charts, diagrams, outlines of Freudian, Marxist, Structuralist and other analyses of the play and all kinds of other notes about the book. By page 149, I have just about finished all the plotting and thinking about how the different characters will analyze *Hamlet*. I have replaced the

Italian critic with an Indian critic, Ishh Uttarpradesh, and the Japanese critic, as well.

On page 193 I find myself speculating about a new murder mystery, and have a chart: B kills A, C kills B, D kills C, E kills D, F kills E, and A kills F. Five years later, I was able to figure out how to write this mystery and wrote *The Mass Comm Murders*. Meanwhile, my *Postmortem for a Postmodernist* was going into production and I was asked to do a reader on postmodernism, and on page 203 of my journal, I'm already listing writers and articles or segments from chapters in books that I might want to consider for the book.

Recently I was reading a book that dealt with postmodernism and literature, which mentioned that many postmodern novels often deal with the trivial aspects of everyday life. That leads me to wonder whether my journals might best be seen as a multi-volume postmodern novel, 94 volumes long and still counting. Each of my journals might be seen as a chapter in a vast, more than fifty years in the making, omni-novel in which I, as an American Everyman, record my thoughts and speculate about all kinds of matters, from meals I've had in restaurants to political concerns. I didn't realize I was writing an autobiographical novel until I started reading what critics had said about postmodernism—a term I was using in the early seventies, it turns out. In the best postmodern tradition, my novel blends genres—the journal and the novel—and has no ending. Not yet, at least, and not for a good long while, I hope.

In addition to giving each journal a title, from journal 30 on I devote the first four pages to a calendar—two months per page—that I use to keep track of what I have to do. On the next page I make a chart of my trips and on the page after that I make a chart of projects. If you look at my journals you see that some projects carry over from journal to journal over a number of years. My journals are full of charts. I make one for a series of book reprints I edit for Transaction Books, another for books I'm thinking of writing. And at the end of my journals I make an index of important ideas and pages in my journal, that I can use in future years to find material I want to look at, for one reason or another. I made a list of these indexes, from journal 30 on, that I can consult when I'm working on some project. I didn't index my journals until number 30.

I also illustrate my journals with little spot drawings, almost invariably with a black background. These drawings give the book a certain amount of visual appeal, but they also help me focus my ideas, from time to time, on some topic. Thus, when I was thinking about writing my mystery on postmodernism, I did a spot drawing that helped me launch the book. It was of Ettore Gnocchi, with his head lying on a table, with a bullet hole in his head, a knife in his back, a poison arrow in his cheek, and a poisonous vapor coming from his spilled drink. Underneath I wrote a paragraph that was to become the first chapter in *Postmortem for a Postmodernist*.

At the end of my journals I also have spaces devoted to books I've read, books I hope to read, royalties, and so on. I only write in my journals in stolen moments, from time to time, each day. But it only takes fifteen minutes of writing each day (almost every day, but not always) to end up with 94 volumes... approximately 20,000 pages.

One of my journals, number 32, was lost. I had forgotten it on a plane coming back from Air France. I had been invited to a conference in France thanks to a friend, Jean-Marie Benoist, who I had met in London when he was the cultural attaché of France there. Though I had my name and address on the first page of the journal, it was sent back to France, to a French professor, Anne-Marie Laulan, who had given me her card and whose card was in the journal. She returned it to me three years later. That explains why I have two journals titled "Relations." When I got the journal back, I changed a new journal I had titled "Relations" to "Relations II." I will admit that when you write as many journals as I have written, sometimes you run out of good idea for titles.

One thing I like about keeping a journal is that journals enable me to discover ideas I "had" but never brought to consciousness...or, in some cases, to think up new ideas. When you are in the process of writing, you find that one idea leads to others and that frequently you end up with something you could not have possibly anticipated when you started writing. It's very similar to writing a book.

When I write my books I generally have an outline of what I'm going to discuss in each chapter, but I find that as I write, new ideas pop into my head and new topics to discuss suddenly suggest themselves, so there is a considerable difference between the chapter as I had envisioned it and what I end up with. This is because, as one writes, various elements of one's unconscious start manifesting themselves. That means that writing is always a process of self-discovery, whatever else it might be, and self-revelation.

I often tell people that I write books to find out what I think about a given subject. And it is in my journals that I do a lot of my thinking—playing around with ideas and speculating about what I should deal with in a given chapter of a book. Sometimes it takes a number of years for some idea I had to become an article or a book and some ideas never move beyond my notes in my journals. It's interesting for me, when I look over my journals, to see how persistent I am and how I often take years to think about some idea for a book before I actually start writing it.

Li'l Abner as a Ph.D. Dissertation Subject

I decided, after my two years in the army and another two years doing this and that (touring Europe, working in New York) that I was most interested in scholarly pursuits and an academic career and in so, in 1960, I went off to the University of Minnesota to work on a Ph.D. in American Studies. When I described the American Studies program at Minnesota to my brother Jason, who is an artist, he told me "American Studies is a Shmoo. If you roast it, you're a literature scholar. If you fry it, you're a historian. If you boil it, you're a sociologist. If you bake it, you're a political theorist. Better to profound yourself in a discipline." Little did I know how significant that reference to Shmoos was to be. The Shmoo was a character in Al Capp's famous comic strip *Li'l Abner.* As Capp described this mythical little beast in his strip, "Fry a Shmoo and it comes out chicken. Broil it and it comes out steak. Shmoo eyes make splendid suspender buttons. Shmoo hide cut thin is fine leather; cut thick, it is the best lumber. Shmoo whiskers make magnificent toothpicks."

I liked American Studies because it allowed me to design a program of study to suit my interests and I thought a multi-disciplinary approach to any topic made a great deal of sense, especially when it came to understanding American culture and society. So I took courses on subjects such as American intellectual history, political theory, social thought, and American literature.

I took a course on American political thought with Mulford Q. Sibley, a professor of political science, that was to lead to my choice of a dissertation topic. He posted a list of possible term paper topics on his door and I chose to write on one of them- -on political aspects of Al Capp's *Li'l Abner*. I chose this topic because I was interested in humor and also in comics. By chance, I had met Al Capp at a party his daughter had in Cambridge a number of years earlier. His daughter was studying art with my brother at the art school of the Museum of Fine Arts in Boston and she told him about her party. And he told me about it. It was in Cambridge. I didn't know it was to be the Al Capp who drew *Li'l Abner* when I went to the party and remember spending a good deal of time chatting with him that night.

Several years after taking that course, I made an appointment to talk with Sibley about my dissertation subject. I thought I might write on Utopian thought, which interested me a great deal and which seemed to be a serious subject that the American Studies graduate council, which evaluated dissertation proposals, would accept. It was made up of professors drawn from the humanities and social sciences. Students (and professors, as well, I believe) in American Studies had an inferiority complex of sorts, since faculty members in traditional disciplines, like English and History, tended to look down on them. This led to graduate students choosing excessively dull and seemingly serious subjects to write their dissertations on.

I walked in to see Sibley with the notion of writing about Utopian thought, a good, solid, dull, academic topic and walked out with *Li'l Abner*. "You've already written on Li'l Abner," he said. "Why not expand that essay you wrote for my American political thought course into your dissertation? I know that you're interested in humor and that you're an artist," he continued. "Take my advice and write on *Li'l Abner*." And so, I walked out of his office with a new dissertation subject, *Li'l Abner*. Sibley, I should add, was a very distinguished scholar and I thought that even though my subject seemed a bit unusual, his prestige would help me get it passed by the panel of professors that evaluated dissertation topic statements.

I submitted a proposal in which I said I wanted to analyze *Li'l Abner* and relate it to American culture, and, as I understand it, the professors from the humanities were outraged—that I would do a dissertation on something as trivial and moronic as a comic strip. They wanted to reject the proposal, but the social scientists on the panel supported my proposal, so I was told me to rewrite my proposal and resubmit it. I went to a literature professor, who was the chair of the American Studies graduate council, and he suggested that I be more specific in my proposal. We chatted for a while and agreed that I would analyze *Li'l Abner* in terms of its language, its narrative structure, its graphic aspects and its satirical nature. So I revised my proposal, using as much of his language as I could remember, and passed it in. To my great relief, it was accepted and so I ended up writing my dissertation on a comic strip, *Li'l Abner*. It was, I believe, the first dissertation written on a comic strip in an American university.

In my dissertation, I explained that the term "Shmoo" is a variation on the Yiddish term "Schmo" or "Schmuck." As I wrote: (1970:115) "The world "Schmoo" is quite probably a modification of the Jewish term Schmo or Schmuck, which means either "fool" ("booby," "nitwit,") or "penis."

I continued my analysis on the next page (1970:116) " The most intriguing thing about the Shmoo, as I see it, is that it is a phallic symbol, and I say this for a number of reasons. The drawing of the Shmoo looks like an erect penis coming from a gigantic scrotum which emerges between two legs. (We might think of it as a wildly reductionist fantastic creature—man reduced to a penis.) Capp also says that "they multiplies wifout th' slightest encouragement," which brings to mind the reproductive function of the penis. Several of the professors on my dissertation committee were amused by my Freudian perspective and others thought I was out of my mind. None of them new Yiddish, of course.

Most of my fellow Ph.D. graduate students in American Studies all laughed when they heard what I was going to write my dissertation on (that's one of the reason I began my *Li'l Abner* with the words, "they laughed when I sat down at the typewriter"). They all had chosen "serious" and "important" subjects and considered my writing on a mere comic strip, something they used to wrap garbage with, quite absurd. Young scholars tend to be very serious about themselves and their work and my fellow graduate students concluded that working on a significant subject, like Turkish American Relations 1895-1905, would be very beneficial to their careers. One of my colleagues wanted to write on "The Failure of the West." He thought big. He ended up with some third rate novelist, and never finished his dissertation, as far as I know.

I interrupted my graduate studies for a year in 1963. I won a Fulbright to Italy and ended up in Milan, to do some research on the popular Italian magazine press—magazines such as *Oggi* and *Epoca* that had huge circulations. I actually did research on these publications and my article on these magazines was published in an Italian social science journal, *Il Mulino*. In my article I expressed amazement at how a very small staff of journalists could publish a weekly that had a huge circulation.

I described these magazines as being like dinosaurs—with gigantic bodies and a brain the size of a pea. One afternoon while listening to the radio, a newscaster mentioned an article by an American sociologist who described Italian weekly magazines as dinosaurs. It seems the Italians were taken with my description of the Italian weeklies as being like dinosaurs.

I taught two courses in American Studies at the University of Milan. One day I asked my students a question. "Who's doing interesting work in Italy on media and popular culture, and they all gave me the same name—Umberto Eco. He taught at the University of Bologna but lived in Milan, so I called him and got to know him. We first met at the Galleria and had a long discussion. We talked about my work on comics and my interest in popular culture. In Italian, comics are called "fumetti," for the puffs of smoke in which the dialogue is placed. Eco was, it turns, very much interested in popular culture and, in particular, in comics. He had recently written (or maybe he was working on) an article on Superman—known in Italy as "The Nembo Kid," because the Italians didn't want to use the word "Superman" due to its connection with fascism. Through Eco I got to know a number of journalists and scholars doing work on comics in Italy and went to various publishers who were putting out collections of comics. I remember one evening, Umberto and a group of other writers came to my little apartment in Milan. One of them asked for some Scotch. "Sorry," I said, "I don't have Scotch. All I have is grappa." Grappa is a very proletarian drink, but it was better than nothing, so they drank Grappa.

I also started studying Italian comics. My boss at the University of Milan, Agostino Lombardo, whose expertise was in American literature, had a journal, *Studi Americani*, and he asked me to write an article for him on Italian and American comics. So I made a comparative study of American and Italian comics that appeared around the same time and had similar kinds of heroes and heroines and published in it his journal. One thing that I discovered was that in the Italian comics, authority was accepted and in the American comics, authority was considered rejected. I also found Italian sociologists who had also written about attitudes towards authority in Italy and whose conclusions were similar to mine. I included some of this material in the first chapter of my dissertation. In this chapter I dealt with popular culture and the comics and defended of the value of studying comics.

What I did when I analyzed comics and other forms of popular culture was to use the standard techniques of literary and cultural analysis, but apply them to what was then known as "sub-literary" texts. I used psychoanalytic theory, I used sociological theory, I used literary criticism methods, but I used them on *Li'l Abner*, a comic strip, not a novel. When I was doing my research on *Li'l Abner*, I noticed that there were countless articles on Henry James and almost nothing on *Li'l Abner*, which was read by several hundred million people each day, all over the world. I was greatly encouraged by the work the Italians were doing in popular culture and in comics and felt it validated my work. When I returned from Italy, I finished my dissertation and graduated from the University of Minnesota in 1965. I got a job teaching at San Francisco State and have taught there ever since, except for a year teaching as a visiting professor at the Annenberg School for Communication at the University of Southern California in 1984. I taught a large class—200 students—on popular culture. While I was in Los Angeles, I invited Stan Lee, an old acquaintance of mine, to give a lecture and he was kind enough to do so.

I can still remember my graduation from the University of Minnesota in 1965. Someone, perhaps the president of the university, announced the name of the person getting his or her doctorate and the subjects of this person's dissertation. After each name and dissertation subject was announced, the audience clapped. The president would read the person's name and subject."James Benson, Molecular Structure of Amino Acids."

People in the audience clapped. "Sally Johnson, American Abolitionists and the Civil War." People in the audience clapped. "Arthur Asa Berger, Li'l Abner: A Study in American Satire." People in the audience laughed. And so the very first thing that happened to me after I got my doctorate and entered academic life was that people laughed at my choice of a dissertation topic. But I was to have the last laugh, for my dissertation was accepted for publication and appeared in 1970 as *Li'l Abner: A Study in American Satire*. It was later reprinted by the University Press of Mississippi in a series of reprints of important works on popular culture. Also, an article I wrote about attitudes on authority in the Italian and American appeared in a distinguished social science journal, *Transaction* (now renamed *Society*) and I was to eventually have a long relationship with the editor of this journal, Irving Louis Horowitz, and publish a number of books on humor, media and popular culture with Transaction publications.

My interest in comics led to work on other forms of popular culture and to the mass media, as well. I have written on advertising, professional wrestling, television shows, fast foods, humor and numerous other aspects of popular culture and everyday life. I once wrote an article that asked "why is popular culture unpopular?" My answer was that it was popular with the masses—and unpopular with certain elites, that looked down upon ordinary people and their tastes. Investigating this subject has been the work of my life and I have spent almost forty years studying the media, popular culture and everyday life, trying to figure out why people feel the way they do about it and what impact it may be having on our lives and our societies.

One wonderful thing about popular culture is that new developments keep happening all the time. Just when you think you've seen everything, something new comes along, like reality television, that blows your mind. And so you've got to get to work and see if you can figure out what is going on.

I should add that popular culture and the media are now considered valid and important subjects, and scholars from many different disciplines are now investigating these subjects. All of a sudden, people realized that popular culture is a kind of culture and culture has become an important subject in the academy. What used to be called popular culture has transmogrified into a "hot" discipline called culture studies, and now everyone (that is, scholars from many disciplines) is getting into the act. Now books on various aspects—one might say all conceivable aspects—of cultural studies are being published in incredible numbers.

Letters

I used to write an enormous number of personal letters. That's how I kept in touch with my friends. I know how many letters I wrote because I keep a record of letters I've written in my journals. Sometimes I'd write fifteen or twenty letters, or even more, in a month. Now, because of e-mail, I hardly write any letters at all. And I hardly get any personal letters, also. The only person who regularly sends me letters is my brother Jason, who used to live in Lisbon and lived in Brookline, Massachusetts before he died a few years ago. He didn't use computers, so he was reduced to writing letters. I also occasionally write to my former professor, Dave Noble, who always answers. I get some sense of what is going on at the University of Minnesota from him. He is now around ninety years old and going strong.

Somehow, I can't help but feel that this dependence on e-mail is not a sign of progress. E-mail letters are, as a rule, dashed off and are seldom memorable. What this means is that we don't have a means of dealing, in depth, with our ideas and our feelings. We communicate our ideas by sending attachments with our articles and book reviews. The price of speed is a kind of alienation from ourselves and those we care about.

My brother said that I write the same letter all the time—about my books and dealing with editors, my family, and little else. He writes the same letters, too—about his forthcoming exhibitions and where he will be painting in the fall (the Algarve) or summer (Normandy), with a few other things thrown in—meals he's had and friends he's visited. It may be that we treasure personal letters because they are expressions of care and affection and because the written word lives on.

Marxism: Being a Double Marxist

Long ago in London Town
Marx turned Hegel upside down
Revealing him as sans-culotte
Oakeshot saved him from that blot,
Restoring quick his balance true
He dressed him up in Tory blue;
This seemed to be for LSE
Dialectical indecency.

[Note: this is an anonymous poem about Michael Oakeshot, who was for a time, head of the London School of Economics, also known as the London Shul of Economics because it has so many Jewish students.]

KARL MARX

I always have said that two of the greatest influences of my life as a scholar were the two Marxes—Karl Marx and Groucho Marx. From Karl Marx I gained an insight into the power of ideas and their relationship to the mode of production and the needs of ruling elements, that is the ruling classes, in any society. You can't read Marx without being struck by the power of his ideas about false consciousness, alienation, and the role of media in capitalist countries. From Groucho Marx I gained a sense of the need for insouciance and absurdity as a balance to the dreary and boring seriousness one finds so often in life and in so many people.

The problem is that Marxist Utopianism was hijacked by various groups of paranoid peasants, who plundered their societies in the name of a socialist philosophy. The Communist societies never seemed able to move beyond the "dictatorship of the proletariat" stage. The joke in these countries went—"We pretend to work and they pretend to pay us." Studies have shown how full of corruption and exploitation they were, until they finally collapsed.

The films of Groucho Marx and his brothers represented an

anarchistic attack on upper class snobbery and pretension that had one important quality—they were very funny. I've always had a touch of both of the Marxes in me, which might explain my difficulties with academic institutions, the U.S. Army, and people who are very serious about themselves.

The problem with Marxism is that Marxist theorists tend to be rather doctrinaire. There are many different kinds of Marxists, of course, and different ones stress different things. But when you read Marxist critics you can be pretty sure you'll read about alienation, base and superstructure, class conflict, false consciousness, ideology, imperialism, manipulation and a few other terms. In a sense, you know what you'll find, all too often, before you start reading. The same applies to Freudian critics, though there have been so many post-Freudian psychoanalytic theorists that you can't be certain what concept a Freudian critic will use. The same applies to all "isms." What is interesting is when media critics apply the basic concepts in their favorite methodology in original and surprising ways.

I write as someone who often uses Marxist theory in analyzing television shows, films, sports and so on. The problem I always face, when using Marxist theory, is how to avoid being doctrinaire. I am not a Marxist in that I don't think that Marx's theory about communism being inevitable makes sense, but I do think he has supplied us with concepts that we can use to analyzing our popular culture and the mass media, and society in general, with a view towards making American democracy stronger.

Massachusetts (The University of)

I went to the University of Massachusetts in Amherst in 1950. I had applied to and been accepted in a number of schools–Bates, Bowdoin, Colby and the University of Massachusetts, but its tuition was fifty dollars a semester and the tuition at the other colleges was several hundred dollars. So in the Fall of 1950 it was off to Amherst, Massachusetts I went, burning, burning. All students had to take four science courses and four social science courses. So I ended up taking courses in bacteriology, geology, botany, sociology, psychology, economics, history, and so on. My psychology teacher, Al Goss, suggested I go to the University of Iowa for my last two years of college, but the idea was too traumatic for me. I did, however, end up going there for my Master's degree. I did very well in economics and my economics teacher suggested I become an economics major.

There were a number of remarkable "characters" at the University of Massachusetts when I was there...between 1950 and 1954. I was an English major, and the two great figures of the English department were Barney Troy and Maxwell Henry Goldberg. Both had large followings. Troy was a somewhat Olympian figure, and looked like one imagines English professors should look. Handsome, WASPy, tweedy...he lived a long life and was of great service to the University, even after he retired, as a trustee. He had a number of devoted followers.

Goldberg was just the opposite—a short, bald, dumpy figure, generally in rumpled clothes...who taught English the way rabbis teach the Torah—word by word and phrase by phrase. He had come to the University of Massachusetts, originally, to study chicken farming (in the best tradition of many Jews) and became seduced by the muse...trading eggs for existentialism. I believe that when he was a student at the University of Massachusetts, Goldberg had attended Ray Torrey's seminars, about which I will have a good deal to say shortly.

I was a Goldberg follower and took many courses from him. He had this notion that English majors could find jobs with progressive companies. When I was a senior I interviewed for a job with one of the progressive companies Goldberg used to talk about...I think it was Vicks chemicals. The interviewer chatted with me for a few minutes and then threw me out, very quickly, asking, as I left, an interesting question–"did you ever think of going on the stage" (that may have led to my becoming a professor and a "performance" artist)?

There was a philosophy professor, named Glick, who actually had been a chicken farmer. He had huge hands and a wonderful homespun style of teaching. I took a number of philosophy courses from Clarence Shute, who would invite his advanced classes over to his house, give them wonderful chocolate cake and coffee (poured from a gorgeous silver coffee service) and play Beethoven and Bach. I remember he once said something I found startling. "I was thinking about my wife, who I've been married to for thirty years," he said, "and the thought occurred to me–who is this strange person that I've been living with? What is she really like?"

I took a number of watercolor courses with Ian MacIver–an alcoholic who drank himself to death. He threw wonderful parties–lots of liquor and beautiful women–that used to last until dawn. I often fell asleep in his apartment and would wake up, somewhat hung over, with a blanket thrown over me. I drew mad scenes on his window shades with watercolors–monsters with knives, strange beasts, and all kinds of other weird things. He was really a good friend...bitter, I think, because his father, Robert MacIver, one of the most distinguished sociologists in America, had not accepted Ian's desire to be an artist. He was a talented man who destroyed himself. I'm glad that I had the opportunity to know him and that I wasn't around to see his sad death.

And then there was Basil Boise Woods or (Wood?) who was a mad librarian...he was a wild character who was always arresting people, which he claimed he could do under some statute, and sending them to the dean (who always let them go). Woods "arrested" me a couple of times, if I remember correctly. Woods often sported hip boots and cruised through the library shushing people and arresting them.

But the most remarkable of the professors on campus at the time was Ray Ethan Torrey, the terror of "Introduction to Botany," which I took in my Freshman year. He was a morphologist in an age of physiology, a political reactionary in an era of liberalism, and a theosophist in an era of rational religion. I took his botany course in the fall semester of 1950, if I recall. It might have been spring. Women were separated and placed on the sides of the large lecture hall; men were in the center. Torrey drew marvelously and his lectures were remarkable performances. He had a biting sense of humor which manifested itself from time to time. I was in sheer terror (like most everyone else) for he had quite a reputation. He attracted large numbers of students who were willing to undergo the ordeal of the botany course because we all recognized that he was a brilliant and original thinker (some of his views were of questionable validity, when it came to things like straightline evolution, etc.) and his course was exciting.

My laboratory section leader was one of his protégésEugene Putala, I believe. He had a great prognathous jaw and silky hair that hung over his forehead. He had gone to Ohio State, to work on a Ph.D. I believe, but didn't like it and returned to the laboratory at the University of Massachusetts. I heard, years later, that he had actually got marriedif so, a triumph of the power of sexuality over what we now would call "new-age" spirituality.

I was Torrey's reader for a period...I can't recall how long it was. Perhaps two years? He had written an esoteric manuscript, dealing with Theosophist beliefs, and it was my duty to read a portion of the manuscript, until Torrey asked me to stop...then he would comment on the material he had read. It was all about "Master KH" (Koot Hoomi?), battles between red capped lamas and black capped lamas in Tibet, etc. etc.

Torrey always started the sessions with a discussion of the latest broadcast of a right-wing conservative radio commentatorFulton Lewis Junior. Torrey absolutely loathed Eleanor Roosevelt and everything she stood for...liberalism, the welfare society, etc. After his discussion of politics, and related concerns, the seminars would start. They took place in the seminar room of the botany building, where gigantic drawings thatTorrey had made were hung...flowers, plants, etc. No women were allowed...I heard that in earlier years, Torrey had offered a seminar for women, also...but he didn't have the energy or time to offer two seminars each week.

Years later I read some of *Isis Unveiled*, by Madame Blavatsky, and could see the source of many of Torrey's concerns. How ironic that he was so profoundly influenced by a woman. He was always saying that for those who had a true spiritual quest, women (and sex) were dangerous snares. Everyone once in a while I would notice that one of the regulars was missing from the group and then, by chance, see him walking hand in hand with some woman. The power of sexuality had manifested itself once more. From what people told me, I understand that Torrey, in his own way, teaching a course that seemed rather marginal and offering seminars that were attended by few, had enormously influenced scores of people.

Why? Because Torrey was, simply put, a remarkable man. His theories of evolution may have been absurd and he may have been rather eccentric in his spiritual and political beliefs, but he had a kind of intensity and honesty that came through. He was a searcher and went where his search led him, whether it was fashionable or not. That kind of integrity could not help but have consequences...and so, if what I remember is correct, many faculty members had been influenced by him.

I once wrote one of his pet phrases ("Why bother with this trivia in a world stagnant with moral degeneration and spiritual paralysis?") on a geology exam. Our professor, "Rocky" Wilson, had promised an essay exam but, instead, gave a 150 question multiple choice exam, and I was furious. So I wrote the phrase on my exam. The results were incredible...the department considered having me thrown out of school (so I was told by a friend of mine, a Nigerian graduate student in the geology department), I had to apologize to all my geology instructors (a woman named Mrs. Rotan, if I remember, was my lab instructor). Nowadays, of course, not an eyebrow would be raised at something as tame as that. But fifty years ago, things were much different.

It is rather ironic that I would have studied botany with a morphologist (I lost his book years ago...much to my regret. As I understand it, he wrote the book with alternating philosophical and spiritual chapters and his publisher then put out two books: the textbook and the book of spiritual and philosophical essays). In any case, by chance I have become a media critic and have been strongly influenced by the work of literary thinkers and critics known as Formalists and Structuralists. One of the seminal books in this area is Vladimir Propp's famous text, *Morphology of the Folktale*. So, almost thirty years after I discovered that larches have deciduous brachyblasts, I fell under the sway of another morphologist, this time a Russian who analyzed fairy tales.

Torrey was probably an anachronism in the science world even when I was studying with him. The moral of my tale is that a brilliant anachronism is of infinitely greater value (to students, to colleagues, to the university, to everyone) than a scholar who may be up on all the latest information but is a runofthemill personality. Torrey died a number of years ago. They don't make them like that anymore—sad to say!

Material Culture: The Objects of My Affection

This is not a
PIPE

I've been interested in material culture—in objects of one sort or another that reflect interesting things about American culture—for many years. Some have suggested that the interesting things I find are in my own mind, and not in the things I analyze. It probably all started in 1962 or 1963 when I was walking down a street in Minneapolis and noticed that what had been an empty lot now had a small building in it. It was my first encounter with golden arches and McDonald's. At the time, hamburgers cost thirteen cents—or something like that. I bought one and ate it.

I spent a bit of time observing the operation. I noticed that the clerks had a set routine of questions they asked, I saw a sign on the side of the building indicating how many people had eaten McDonald's hamburgers since it was founded, and I couldn't help but wonder about the symbolism of the golden arches.

I concluded that McDonald's had the same dynamics of evangelical Protestant churches and wrote an article for *The Minnesota Daily* titled "The Evangelical Hamburger." I saw ritual, I saw religious symbolism in the arches, I saw (in the sign) membership in a group or congregation that is constantly growing, and thus argued that McDonald's hamburgers symbolized something of enormous importance. The article caused a bit of a scandal, since a number of people in Minneapolis thought it was sacrilegious.

Many years later the idea of analyzing American culture by examining the objects and rituals that are part of our everyday lives occurred to me. I had the idea of writing a book, to be called *Ulysses Sociologica*, which would take one day in the life of a typical American, and analyze every object and ritual, considering them to be signs and therefore holding meaning and significance. I hoped to write an analytical book that dealt with a person in much the same way that Joyce wrote a novel about one day in Leopold Bloom's life. I couldn't do a whole day but I did one morning's objects and rituals, for my hero, also named Bloom, and wrote a book that was published as *Bloom's Morning*.

In this book I analyze such things as clock radios, king sized beds, razors, toasters, trash compactors, gel toothpaste, underwear...and so on. Each of my essays is relatively short and in each I always strive to uncover some hidden or unrecognized significance to the object. The idea of dealing with material culture is not new. Malinowski dealt with it in his book on the Trobiand Islanders fifty years ago. Barthes did it in *Mythologies*. And there now are journals devoted to the subject. The hard part is moving from a recognition that objects can be seen as signs and therefore are meaningful to find the right objects to analyzing and interpreting the meanings in these objects. That's the hard part.

I must confess to having a bit of fun in *Bloom's Morning*, which has led some people to think that the book is a big put-on! For example, in my analysis of toasters I discuss toast from a philosophical point of view. I write,

> "What is toast—the product of a process or the process itself? That is, does bread become toast (and change its identity somehow), or do we toast bread and thereby only modify its character slightly? Is toast bread that has been processed (toasted) or changed (made into toast)?"

I wrote my analysis before the phrase "I'm toast" or "You're toast" became popular. Why toast has come to mean failure is something of which the meaning and significance I haven't yet figured out. It seems to me, based on my analysis of toasters and toast, people who use these phrases about toast, who seem themselves as toast (which is what the metaphor "I'm toast" suggests) believe implicitly in the notion that toast is something that has been changed considerably. But why toast means failure is another matter.

I now see this book as one of my postmodern efforts, for there is an element of irony, of the "put-on," and of game playing in *Bloom's Morning*. The fact that this book was published, as I suggested earlier, made me believe in miracles. It was translated into German, which made me think that had I been born and educated in Europe, I would have had a much easier time of things. It has also been published in China, which strikes me as quite remarkable. God only knows what the Chinese who read my book will think about the United States of America.

Media Gurus, Communication Theorists and Pop Culturists I have Known

Umberto Eco: Semiotician, Pop Culturist, Novelist

In 1963 I had a Fulbright to Italy. Since I had proposed doing some research on Italian weekly magazines, I was sent to Milan. I taught two courses at the University of Milan (my boss was Agostino Lombardo) and conducted my research–which eventuated in an article in *Il Mulino*, an Italian scholarly journal.

UM BERTO   ECO

My students in Milan had told me that the most interesting person I might meet in Milan was Umberto Eco. At that stage in his development, Eco was a semiotician writing about popular culture. So was I, it turned out. I called Eco on the phone and we agreed to meet in the Galleria there for a coffee. We found that we both were doing work on the comics and had other similar interests—in media and popular culture.

This was, we must remember, before Eco had written his novels and had become a multi-millionaire. I remember his as a short, bearded, and quite friendly person. He invited me and my wife to his house, later that year, and I recall that his house was full of books of comics and books about the comics. He had a bunch of recorders and played the recorder quite well. I'm not sure, but Eco may have been the person translating *Peanuts* into Italian. Or, perhaps, it was a friend of his. In any case, he was a nationally known figure who was very interested in popular culture; his work on popular culture and the work of various other Italian scholars made me believe that it was a legitimate–and important- subject, even though American scholars generally found it trivial and not worth bothering with. I recall being at a conference at Stanford University and a very well-known and highly regarded sociologist, Melvin Temin, from Princeton, told me he thought popular culture was worth a half an hour at most in his courses.

Eco hung around with a group of intellectuals who

were obsessed with media. I recall one night that Eco, Furio Columbo and a group of editors and architects came over to my apartment for drinks one night. It was quite interesting listening to their impassioned discussions of Dr. Kildare. "Perfect as far as technique is concerned, with brilliant acting", the adventures of Superman, and so on. They stayed until midnight. The conversation was quite lively at times…working itself up into a crescendo and then falling. They had some excellent jokes, too.

A few weeks after that, Umberto invited me to a party one of his friends, an architect, was giving…in a beautiful large (10 or 12 rooms) apartment in Milan. We stayed until 2:00 A.M. A thick fog had come in. When we left we found our car; I went across the street to start it so I could circle around and pick up my wife. I heard my wife screaming "Arthur, Arthur." I looked and saw that some police had grabbed my wife and wanted to push her into a van. They thought she was a street walker. I ran across the street screaming "my wife, my wife." They realized their mistake and let my wife go (she's a philosopher with a particular interest in ethics).

A number of years ago Eco was brought to California by the University of California at Berkeley and Stanford. He got in touch and was kind enough to give a couple of lectures at San Francisco State University, as a personal favor.

In the last thirty years Umberto Eco has gained a considerable amount of weight and now is, physically, a much more substantial figure. I understand he's had heart trouble. I saw him last at an International Semiotics meeting held at the University of California at Berkeley. He gave me a big hug and asked how things were going. A million people were trying to get at him—for interviews, to show him manuscripts, etc. It sort of reminded me of Woody Allen's character in *Stardust Memories*—hounded by all sorts of people hoping to cash in on him.

Eco now has a big house in Milan—a mansion with 30,000 books in it. I don't know how much time he gets to spend in it because he gives so many lectures and appears at conferences all over the world. But he must be around some of the time in it because he still manages to write a great deal on media, popular culture, semiotics and various other topics. And he comes out with a large new novel regularly. I wrote a comic poem in poor

Italian about him that goes more or less as follows (I can't find the poem and I've forgotten the Italian I knew):

> Umberto Eco, scritt(am)ore
> Fa due cose con furore.
> Ogni anni, com macchini
> Esche due libri e bambini.

He has many honorary doctorates from the most prestigious universities and remains one of the most important semioticans and culture theoristsand novelists... of the day.

Marshall McLuhan: Media Guru and Visionary

In 1965 or around then Marshall McLuhan was in San Francisco, spending time with a famous advertising executive and, as we say, "making the scene." I read in Herb Caen's column that McLuhan was in town and called the advertising agency where he was staying and asked if I might have the opportunity to chat with him. To my great surprise and pleasure, I was invited over to the agency, where the advertising executive and some friends (a doctor named Gerald Feigen, if I recall correctly, who communicated with kids by using a puppet, etc.) were sitting around.

McLuhan was, at the time, very famous. The press was crazy about him, though many academics found his style of writing too jazzy for them. A number of scholars thought he was extremely perceptive and interesting while others considered him something of a charlatan. He had been taking a nap and came down a few minutes after I arrived. He had finely drawn features and a head of wavy gray hair, if I recall correctly.

What was interesting, to me, is that I found it almost impossible to carry on a normal conversation with him. It was like something out of *Finnegan's Wake*...his mind seemed to have been racing ahead four or five steps beyond where our conversation was at the time. I wasn't quite sure how to talk with him...but he seemed genuinely interested in talking with me and encouraging me on with my work on popular culture.

Topless dancing was very popular in San Francisco and I told McLuhan I was interested in the phenomenon. He suggested I investigate the matter and write something on it, which I did. I visited a number of Topless bars, interviewed some topless dancers (not topless when I interviewed them), managers of the bars, bartenders, etc. and wrote an essay on what topless reflected about American culture and society. I interviewed Carol Doda, at the time the most famous of the topless dancers in San Francisco (thanks to Herb Caen) and another dancer who could make each of her breasts revolve in a different direction at the same time. My essay was published in *The Journal of Popular Culture*. This topic was, as we say in America, quite a challenge. "It's tough work analyzing popular culture–but somebody's got to do it."

A number of years later I wrote a book on American television (with a few chapters devoted to British television). McLuhan was kind enough to write an introduction for the book, which must have been difficult–since he argued "the medium is the message" and my book consisted of analyses of various television programs such as *Mission Impossible, Star Trek, All in the Family* and *Kung Fu*. I was interested in the message but he managed to write a gracious introduction.

McLuhan's reputation took a nose-dive and in recent years I've actually had reviewers of some of my book manuscripts (for my publisher) attack me for including anything from McLuhan in them. Now, the tide has turned and he is getting increasing respect.

McLuhan was a literature professor who saw, very early, how important comics and advertising were and discussed them in one of his most important books, a book I consider to be a classic of popular culture analysis (now it would be described as a Cultural Studies book), *The Mechanical Bride*. McLuhan repudiated this book because it focused on the content of media instead of the media themselves–the subject of his best known book, *Understanding Media*.

A wonderful new book, Donald F. Theall's *The Virtual Marshall McLuhan*, explains what McLuhan was doing. Theall writes:

> McLuhan became frustrated trying to teach first year
> students in required courses how to read English poetry,

and began using the technique of analyzing the front page of newspapers, comic strips, ads, and the like as poems— applying the new critical techniques he had encountered in the Cambridge school as interpreted through his sense of the history of literature and rhetorical expression and expressed in a histrionic stance reinforced by his natural wit. This new approach to the study of popular culture and popular art forms led to his first major move towards new media and communication and eventually resulted in his first book, *The Mechanical Bride*, which some consider to be one of the founding documents of early cultural studies. While *The Bride* was not initially a success, it introduced one aspect of McLuhan's basic method—using poetic methods of analysis in a quasi-poetic style to analyze popular culture phenomena...*The Bride* illustrated yet another aspect of the ongoing McLuhanesque approach to cultural phenomena—the satiric use of wit and the comic as a mode of "tweaking" hidden levels of meaning and complexity from material that seems to be relatively simple—*Blondie, Li'l Abner*, the front page of a Hearst tabloid, ads for caskets, laundry soap, or stockings. (pp. 4,5)

When I read this I recognized, immediately, how much I had learned from reading *The Mechanical Bride* and how similar, in many respects, my interests (and methods of analysis) and McLuhan's were.

Elihu Katz: Media Sociologist and Torah Scholar

In 1984 I was a visiting professor at the Annenberg School of Communications (now "for" Communications) at the University of Southern California in Los Angeles. I taught a huge course (200 students) on popular culture, media and related concerns. I'm proud to say that I taught a number of members of the football team, the wrestling team, and the baseball team more than they wanted to know about semiotics, psychoanalytic theory, and Marxist theory.

The Annenberg School found me an apartment where they had placed two other visiting professors, Daniel Dayan, the French semiotician, and Elihu Katz, the Israeli (born in America) media sociologist. The two spent a great deal of time together and were working on a book on media events that was later to be published by the Harvard University Press. I joined the two of them together–as far as their names were concerned–calling them "Danielihu." We lived at an apartment complex called The Oakwood Apartments.

To me, Los Angles was a horror. I had come from a beautiful little town just a few miles north of the Golden Gate Bridge, Mill Valley, where I had my own house and a gorgeous view. I was plunked down at Third and Vermont Streets, in the middle of an expensive (but crummy) apartment complex in a rather unpleasant section of Los Angeles. It was about thirty blocks north of the USC campus–which is why the Oakwood Apartments were chosen. Elihu seemed impervious to the place; in part, no doubt, because he was invited here and there all the time, so he wasn't around that much.

Daniel Dayan told me a wonderful story that characterizes Elihu. "Two planes crash in the middle of the Atlantic. And Elihu Katz is on *both* of them!"

Elihu is short, has a head of frizzy gray hair (combed to cover a bald spot), and a somewhat bulbous nose. He has a very engaging smile and is quite friendly and interested in all kinds of things. His wife Ruth thinks that Elihu made a mistake getting involved with the media. As she said to me, during a visit to Los Angeles, "I don't know why Elihu left conventional sociology and got involved with mass communications and the media."

This remark reflects a sense that many scholars have that communications, media studies, etc. is not really a "legitimate" scholarly field (this probably has changed with the development of Cultural Studies; now everyone wants to get into the act and analyze media, teach courses on comics, detective novels, etc.). Katz has an international reputation and was one of the "stars" in the Annenberg galaxy of big-name professors. One day I suggested to him that we study the Torah–the first five books of the Old Testament–together. And so we began a fairly regular class studying the Torah–and having coffee and cake afterwards. Elihu would read the Hebrew and translate and then Daniel, assorted visitors and guests, my wife and I would discuss the passage and argue about it, in the best tradition of studying the Torah. I had managed, somehow, to set up a part-time Yeshiva at the Oakwood Apartments.

While at the Annenberg I suggested (half jesting, that is) that the inner court of the building be turned into a restaurant–to be called Chez Walter, after Walter Annenberg, who provided funds for the school. This area was used for various parties and social events the school sponsored, so I figured why not turn it into a restaurant? Curiously enough I've heard that the inner court of the building actually will be turned into a coffee shop or restaurant, after all. But it won't be called Chez Walter. More likely Starbucks or some fast food emporium.

The last time I saw Elihu was when my wife and I traveled in Israel in the Summer of 1990(?). Elihu and Ruth picked us up at our hotel and took us to a marvelous "Oriental" restaurant (Moroccan or something in that general genre) where we had a superb dinner and lots of fun talking about our days together at the Annenberg School.

Elihu left the Annenberg School for Communications at the University of Southern California and joined the Annenberg School for Communications at the University of Pennsylvania, where he teaches–as I understand it–when not at The Hebrew University in Jerusalem.

Pea Soup and Sausages with Karl Erik, the Chartmeister of Lund University

In the Fall of 1996 I had a sabbatical and spent some time giving lectures and workshops in Denmark and Sweden. This lecture tour was set up by Kim Shroder, who I met at the Annenberg School when I taught there. I was going to be in Portugal, visiting my brother–a landscape painter who lives in Lisbon–so it was just a short airplane ride to Copenhagen, where I spent some time lecturing at various faculties and, in some cases, conducting workshops on humor.

One of the places I went was the University of Lund, just a short ferry ride and train ride from Copenhagen. I gave a workshop there on Thursday, Oct. 6, 1994. I had met Karl Erik Rosengren a few years or so before, at an International Communication Association meeting. Perhaps it was in Hawaii?

In any case, he has a nicely trimmed beard, short hair and large glasses. He arranged for a number of his colleagues to get together and for me to offer a workshop on humor. I mentioned earlier one of my books, *An Anatomy of Humor*, in which I argue that there are 45 techniques that humorists use to generate laughter–often using a number of techniques at the same time. The humorists aren't aware of what they are doing but I've "deconstructed" (one might say) humor and can show, with any example of humor, which techniques are at work.

I provided everyone at the workshop with a sheet with a chart of the 45 techniques listed by category and another chart in which the techniques are numbered in alphabetical order. These charts are found earlier in this book, in my discussion of humor. I also had a number of jokes for my "students" to deconstruct. I use jokes because they are short texts and are often quite complex, employing two or three (and sometimes more) techniques. I argue, I should point out, that one should never tell jokes to be funny because people may have heard them, because most people don't tell jokes well, and because telling a joke (a short narrative meant to amuse with a punch line) is an exercise in performing other people's material.

In any case, Karl Erik was there and so was Phil Tichenor, a visiting professor from Minnesota, and a few other colleagues from Lund as well. I put them into teams of three and asked them to list the numbers and techniques of six or eight jokes that I gave them. What interested me is that when I do this with my students, they are able to list the techniques quite rapidly. Not so with Karl Erik and his colleagues. Their minds are so complicated that they spun all kinds of wild applications of the techniques. I marveled, as I listened to the groups talk, at how they were able to take something relatively simple and turn it into something astoundingly complex. And at how they screwed up, terribly. It was actually very funny.

Later, Karl Erik took Phil and me to a lovely restaurant where we had pea soup and a sausage. In Sweden it seems that Thursdays everyone has pea soup and I was there on a Thursday. In 1973 I also gave some lectures in Sweden, also at Lund University (but for a Folklorist, Nils Bringeus whose claim to fame is that he has investigated what people do with the last slice of bread in a loaf of bread) and I was there on a Thursday, so I also had pea soup. All I ever had to eat in Sweden, until I visited Goteborg University, was pea soup. My visit to Goteborg was not on a Thursday, but on the following Tuesday, so I had the chance to eat something else.

I had the opportunity to give talks at a number of Danish and Swedish universities and was impressed, let me add, at the work they are doing. Communication studies is very advanced in these countries and there are a number of younger scholars who are doing exciting work.

Karl Erik Rosengren is, of course, one of the most important media theorists and scholars of the present day and his papers are characterized by all kinds of ingenious charts and diagrams. He gave me several of his papers and I was astonished by his creativity in thinking up charts, diagrams, tables and so on...that help explain how the communication process works. He is, I would say, the very model of a modern communications scholar.

A Visitor Who Wandered Into Communication Studies

I was not trained in communications; my Ph.D. is in American Studies, as I've explained earlier, and I wrote my dissertation at the University of Minnesota under the direction of a political theorist, Mulford Q. Sibley. But I wrote it on the comic strip *Li'l Abner* and that sparked my interest in popular culture–in the broadest sense of the term. I wrote articles on McDonald's Hamburgers ("The Evangelical Hamburger") arguing that its dynamics were those of an evangelical religion. I wrote on professional (that is "fake") wrestling as the political science of the ordinary man and woman (little did I know, at the time, that a professional wrestler would become governor of Minnesota). I wrote on comic strips, television, material culture, semiotics and various other topics that suggested themselves to me, as I found myself lost in that wilderness we know as communications, media studies, mass communications, mass media and now, cultural studies.

It was George Gerbner, then Dean at the Annenberg School of Communications at the University of Pennsylvania, who convinced me I was a Communications scholar. "Your field is Communications," he told me, when I said I was thinking of, perhaps, going back into American Studies. Or maybe Communications teacher or writer would be more accurate, since some people don't consider me a scholar—whatever that is.

My interest in popular culture led me into investigating

those aspects of the media and of American culture and society that interested me and into learning various methodologies for analyzing media. I see myself as essentially a textual critic who, along the way, while wandering in the wilderness, has written on a number of related topics. The question in my mind is–will I ever get out of the wilderness?

Wilbur Schramm said that communications is a field where many meet but few linger. He probably was right, but more and more scholars seem to be lingering for longer and longer periods. In my case, I've lingered for almost forty years. I've had the good fortune to meet, as I wandered about, some very interesting people–a few of whom I've described in this brief memoir (I also spent a Summer as a Summer camp working with John Updike, when he was at Harvard and before he became a celebrated novelist—but he's not a communication theorist so I've not dealt with him).

But I think, after nearly 40 years in the wilderness of media studies, communication theory, and so on, and more than forty books, I finally see the light at the end of the tunnel. And light, of course, can be seen as facilitating communication and even, in some cases, as communication. The light at the end of the tunnel I see most often, however, is the one a few miles after the northern end of the Golden Gate Bridge leading to Mill Valley and Marin County, where I live now, in semi-retirement. Note: This selecction draws on an article I published about my meetings with various media theorists.

Minnesota

After almost two years in the Army, a year making the great tour of Europe, and a year working at odd jobs in New York (for six months I worked for the Seafarers International Union), I went off to the University of Minnesota. I was accepted but wasn't given a grant, so I ended up teaching bonehead English and later other courses. It was there that I met two of the most important influences on my intellectual development and on my style of teaching. These teachers were Mulford Q. Sibley and David Noble.

Mulford Q. Sibley was a political theorist and a thorn in the side of all the conservatives in Minneapolis and St. Paul. Sibley was a socialist and an anarchist, who led many marches against the Vietnam War (in which I participated) and spoke out, courageously, against it. He was also a superb scholar and a wonderful teacher. I took so many courses with him that my advisor in the American Studies program prohibited me from taking any other courses he taught.

He passed out a series of several dozen study questions, and used two or three of them (sometimes mixing parts of different questions together) in the essay examinations we took. These study questions helped us read the text we were assigned and focus our attention on important matters. When we got near the exam, Sibley would often eliminate a few questions, so we were usually left with around a dozen questions to answer in preparation for his exams. At the time he was working on a history of political thought, and every class period he would come in with a manila folder in which he had his lecture notes. He was a marvelous lecturer. He was very well organized and enabled us to see how political thought had evolved over the centuries as political thinkers grappled with various problems. He could easily have taught in a philosophy department, since political theory really is political philosophy.

Sibley had a large following at the University of Minnesota and his classes were large, but he made the subject matter so interesting that you never were conscious of being in a huge class. He was very patient about answering questions but managed, still, to carry out his program of lecturing and keep up with his schedule. He also had a wonderful wry sense of humor which made his lectures entertaining.

He asked us to do interesting and imaginative term papers. He circulated a list of topics that we might want to consider, and some of his topics were most unusual. For example, in one of his courses, I believe it was American political thought, he listed "The social and political aspects of *Li'l Abner*" as one of the topics to be investigated. I wrote a paper on this topic and later on wrote my dissertation, under Sibley's direction, on this subject. I had an appointment with him one afternoon- to discuss my dissertation subject. I walked in thinking about doing something on a serious subject like Utopias and walked out with a comic strip—*Li'l Abner*.

As I wrote in one of my journals, "Sibley is one of the finest teachers I've ever had and one of the finest people I've ever met" (do the two generally go together?). His presence pervaded the University of Minnesota and his influence radiated out from it, all over the state. He also had the virtue of laughing at my jokes and puns.

David Noble was the other important influence on my life. I studied intellectual history with him and had I not done my dissertation with Sibley, I would have done it with Noble. He had suggested that I write on the politics of American humor, a subject that interested me but that seemed a bit too amorphous. Noble had a wonderful style of lecturing and was very popular. Hundreds of students used to take his courses in American Intellectual History. He had a very distinctive perspective on things and also had a flair for dramatizing his lectures. Eventually he got the idea of taking on the personae of some of his characters and not only acted like them but "played" them in his lectures. He would dress the part, too.

As a result of back trouble, he had trouble sitting, and could only stand or lie on his back. He took to writing, while lying on his back, and ended up being an extremely productive author, publishing a number of important books on American intellectual history. I got to know him very well, and have corresponded with him since 1965, when I graduated from Minnesota. From time to time, in this correspondence, I used to write comic poems about Noble and we traded titles of books that were of interest and wrote about things in general. From Noble I picked up the notion that it is useful to "dramatize" ideas and beliefs and that having a "style" or perspective on things is important. In one of his lectures, I remember, he took on the persona of Dwight MacDonald and gave a lecture as MacDonald, reading from his books (lots of juicy sexual material) and offering what I thought was a bravura performance. He got a lot of applause. As I was leaving the classroom I overheard two young women talking about Noble. "He's getting worse and worse," one of them said, shaking her head.

I wrote a parody of a Puritan funeral elegy about Noble that I included in a hundred page essay (single spacing, though with drawings) I once wrote to him, which I called *The Recapitulation..*

Anagram on David Noble's Lamentable Death

> David Noble
> Avid Blonde
> Though colorless, yet must you dye
> And be brought low, though you were never high.
> Thy life, not short amongst this earthly throng,
> Was held, by all who knew you, far too long.

I had, by chance, created an identity for myself as an academic "secret agent" and have used it for years to good effect. I had been asked by George Gerbner, Dean of the Annenberg School of Communication at the University of Pennsylvania, for an article on popular culture. He junked most of it, but kept one section called "The Secret Agent." So I played with the identity. Students can understand what a secret agent does and can, at least, follow me when I suggest that I search for secrets that are hidden in media, popular culture and everyday life.

At Minnesota I also studied with Ralph Ross, who taught courses on social and political thought from a position in the Humanities department. He had the ability to come in for a three hour seminar and, without a scrap of paper in front of him, lead discussions and speak brilliantly, about important philosophers and their ideas. I always marveled at his range of knowledge and wondered why it was he never became a figure of national prominence.

Brand Blanchard was a visiting professor who had, I believe, retired from Yale. He taught a course in philosophy and was a superb teacher. It was said that before every lecture he was busy rewriting and revising his notes. His lectures showed it: they were very well organized and masterfully delivered...full of detail, anticipating objections to ideas (and dealing with them), incisive, devastating in their attacks, and witty as well.

I took a course in creative writing from Allen Tate. The University of Minnesota had a policy of having an important writer on the faculty of the English department and when Robert Penn Warren left Minnesota for Yale, Allen Tate was brought in. We read *The Good Soldier* and a few other novels in his writing class, and he talked a great deal about the craft of writing. He dressed beautifully and used to have the class to his house for parties from time to time. I always remember him as friendly but somehow distant.

I also studied with Brom Weber, an obsessively sardonic and sarcastic individual who was interested in American humor and edited a volume on that subject. I was his assistant in a course on the historical development American humor and remember how he taught: he had a stack of note cards that he brought with him to class and he went through them, one by one. He tended to lecture in a monotone and could be rather tiring. Yet, he was extremely funny at times...especially when he got onto the subject of education ("give the students a degree when they enter, so we don't have to bother with exams they don't study for and term papers they plagiarize, and the students can just party for four years without distractions") or, after he had moved to the University of California at Davis, the English department at Minnesota and various professors in it. He had no love for the people running the department at Minnesota who, he believed, had forced him out and who had destroyed what had once been a great department. He was probably right.

It's hard to know precisely what it is that we learn from teachers. From some we get important information, but I think there's more to it than that. After all, we forget most of what we learn in our courses—unless we have reason to use this material for one reason or another. So what you learn from teachers seems to be more a matter of being exposed to different personalities, to people with different perspectives on things–with unusual ideas, with "strange" methods of analysis, with different styles of presenting their ideas and themselves to others. And from all this we develop our own ways of teaching. That's why I think that distance learning can never replace the experience of being in a classroom with a teacher and other students, even if distance learning can "simulate" the experience, to a certain degree.

It was while I was studying at the University of Minnesota that I met a beautiful young woman named Phyllis Wolfson, who was working on a Master's Degree in Philosophy. Six months after meeting her we got married—the best decision I ever made, and I'd like to think, the best decision that she ever made. I even got her to write, in one of my journals, in a moment of weakness, "Marrying Arthur was the best decision I ever made."

My Mysteries

In recent years, as I've mentioned from time to time in this book, I have been writing what might be described as comic academic mysteries that also function as textbooks. They might be thought of as FICTexts or MYSTexts. What they do is teach readers about some subject, but this teaching is "hidden," so to speak, in a work of fiction that takes the form of a far-fetched mystery story. It all started when Mitch Allen, the president of AltaMira Press, asked me to do a comic book on postmodernism. I'm an artist as well as a writer and he thought I might do a comic book that would also function as a text book.

I found that I simply couldn't do the comic book. The format was too limiting for me, but I happened on the idea of writing a humorous mystery novel instead of a comic book that would teach readers about postmodernism. And so I wrote *Postmortem for a Postmodernist*. I also illustrated the book with comicstrip frames at the beginning of each chapter and included quotations from well-known theorists, relevant to postmodernism, before each chapter.

For those interested in the creative process, let me describe what happened when I first got the idea of writing a mystery instead of doing a comic book. I was writing in my journal—as I explained earlier, I've been keeping a journal since 1956—and an image popped into my head. It was of a man slumped over a table. The man had a bullet hole in the middle of his forehead, a knife sticking out of his back, a poison dart in his cheek, and a glass of wine he'd been drinking from had spilled over, with toxic fumes (from poison) emanating from it. That is, he'd been murdered four different ways.

This was to be the first chapter in my book. I also drew a comicstrip frame with Gnocchi slumped over that was to go on the first page. I then created an international cast of bizarre characters.

Ettore Gnocchi...the father of American postmodernism and University Professor at the University of California in Berkeley. Was he the kindly, lovable man he was supposed to be or was he really a monstrous sexual predator who used his power as a University Professor to cater to his insatiable needs? He was having a dinner party at his house with a group of colleagues who were helping him put on a conference on postmodernism. Each person at the dinner party had a good reason to hate Gnocchi. That might explain why he was killed four different ways. But how come he was killed at the same moment in time?

Shoshana TelAviv...Gnocchi's still beautiful Israeli wife... also a postmodernist and also a professor at Berkeley. Did she know about Gnocchi's numerous liaisons, and if she did know, did she care? What exactly was her relationship with Gnocchi? Was she having an affair with Alain Fess? And what was Slavomir Propp's hand doing on her knee during the dinner party the evening that Gnocchi was murdered?

Alain Fess...a "brilliant" young philosopher from France who had written one important book on postmodernism. Then his career suddenly stalled? Fess wrote his dissertation under Gnocchi and barely survived the experience. There were rumors that Fess was sleeping with Shoshana TelAviv. Would it have been convenient for Fess if Gnocchi were, somehow, put out of the way?

Slavomir Propp...a fat Russian linguist and postmodernist, who loved to eat and had an excellent recipe for cheesecake. What was his hand doing on Shoshana TelAviv's knee at the dinner party the evening Gnocchi was murdered? Gnocchi, according to Propp, stole his ideas and published them in one of Gnocchi's most acclaimed books. Was this true? If so, why was Propp working with Gnocchi and the others to put on a conference on postmodernism?

Myra Prail...the most recent of a long list of beautiful graduate students who were Gnocchi's research assistants. She was also doing her dissertation under his supervision. Was she working under Gnocchi in other ways? Did she have very round heels, as Miyako Fuji suggested? Or was Myra Prail a determined woman who would do anything to get ahead and who knew exactly what she was doing?

Basil Constant...an English writer whose novels were considered minor classics in the postmodernist literary canon. Was he gay or bisexual? Did it matter? There were wild rumors that he was actually Thomas Pynchon. Could that be possible? What was Constant doing at Berkeley with a group of academics since he loathed students and professors? Did he have any designs on anyone? Myra Prail was using his novels in her dissertation. Was there anything funny about that?

Miyako Fuji...a stylish professor of philosophy from the University of Tokyo. Gnocchi had been her dissertation advisor. She loathed Gnocchi. She hated him but she came to America to help him put on his conference. Why was her behavior so eccentric? Why did she stare at people at times? And what was her relationship to Alain Fess? She had made a postmodernist film. How did it reflect the postmodernist sensibility? Was there such a thing as postmodernism and a postmodernist aesthetic or was postmodernism anything you could get away with?

Solomon Hunter...an enigmatic police inspector. He seemed rather uninteresting, and not particularly clever. Was that a pose? Does that explain why everyone who was at the dinner party was terrified of him. Or was it because nobody could figure him out, could "read" him? Hunter got an earful on postmodernism while he tried to figure out who killed Gnocchi. Did postmodernism somehow help answer to the question-who killed Ettore Gnocchi? Does postmodernism answer any other questions?

These characters all contradict one another about what happened, give different interpretations of postmodernism when they are interrogated by Hunter, are involved with love and hate relationships with one another, and spoof academic life. I had to figure out how to carry the story forward and, at the same time, put in enough material about postmodernism to teach readers something about the subject.

The book has had a modest success and has had a number of printings. In addition, it has been translated into Chinese, so Chinese students of postmodernism can now follow the adventures of Ettore Gnocchi and all the other characters in their own language. The Chinese used my mystery to create what we would call here a coffee-table art book, full of photographs, paintings, drawings and other illustrations, many in color, reflecting the postmodern sensibility. I think it was quite a remarkable idea and it is a truly beautiful book.

I had so much fun writing the book that I decided to try my hand at some other mysteries. My next book was one

I called *The Hamlet Case: The Murders at the Modern Language Association* meeting. It was published by Xlibris. com, a publisher of "print-on-demand" books, because I couldn't find a publisher to take a chance on it. In this book I have a number of strange literature professors, with different orientations to literature, analyze *Hamlet*. They are all killed by a crazed literature professor from the University of California, Agostino Glioma, but not before each of them offers a different interpretation of Hamlet. Readers of this book will get a psychoanalytic interpretation, a structuralist interpretation, a Marxist interpretation, a Feminist interpretation, a historical interpretation, and a literary theorist's interpretation of the play.

The first chapter of my comic mystery *The Hamlet Case* reads as follows:

It was I who drove a hatchet into the head of that castrating bitch, the feminist critic Anastasia Spivak-Trotsky. And it was I who shot that pseudo-Marxist fraud, the critic Boris Jameson-Kellnerov. And it was I who blew a poison dart into the neck of that monstrous bore, the Indian structuralist critic, Ishh Uttarpradesh. And it was I who, with a plastic bomb, blew up that the literary theorist, Anne-Sophie Kristena and at the same time, with a stroke of luck, that naive crank, the Freudian critic, Melanie JungFreud and the sociological critic, Clive Barker, who were both in bed with her in a disgusting ménage a trios. By my good fortune I killed three persons at the same time, which means, and this is perhaps an absurd legalism, I am not and should most certainly not be thought of as–whatever else I may be–a serial killer.

Here is a part of the second chapter, which will give you a better idea of what the book is about and the style in which the book is written.

My name is Agostino Glioma and I am Edward Devere professor of literature at the University of California in Berkeley, which is not, by any means, as great a university as it thinks it is, except, perhaps, in the sciences and engineering. I am, and have been for thirty years, editor of Shakespeare Studies, a scholarly journal devoted to Shakespeare's works–arguably, the most interesting and brilliant poems and plays ever written. The journal publishes articles on all matters relating to Shakespeare, including Shakespeare's life, performances of his plays and the way they have been staged, criticism of his work, and all books, plays, and other texts connected to him in any way, in any language.

The people whom I killed were all members of the editorial board of the journal and simply had to be eliminated. That's because they wanted to eliminate me...that is, replace me as editor. And they wanted to include all kind of trendy trash in Shakespeare Studies, intellectual garbage by academic hacks–careerists and morons who wanted to use Shakespeare to further their own petty ambitions. I would have none of it. But I could not prevent them from getting their way, a good deal of the time, about the articles we published. Finally, when the journal had become a travesty of scholarship, full of articles by Feminists and postmodernists, and the threat to my editorship was about to manifest itself, I decided, secretly, on a course of action and, like Hamlet, "taking arms against a sea of trouble," I decided to get rid of each of them in a suitable way.

I am waiting for Inspector Solomon Hunter of the San Francisco police department to come and arrest me. Last night he called and said he wanted to speak with me...I'm sure he knows that I, Agostino Glioma, holder of the Edward Devere Chair of literature at Berkeley, am the mysterious murderer he's been looking for these past few days. He reached this conclusion by a simple process of elimination. I am the only person alive from the editorial board of Shakespeare Studies.

I think you can see what my comic mystery textbooks are like. They use exaggeration, stereotyping, insult, facetiousness and various other techniques of humor to amuse readers and get them to keep turning the pages, a most important matter for any writer. One of the wonderful things about novels is that you can create dialogues among characters and "pump" content into these dialogues.

In *Durkheim is Dead* I wrote a Sherlock Holmes mystery that was also a textbook on sociological theory. My last mystery was *Mistake in Identity* on the subject of identity.

NOSES MAY NOT EXIST !!

THE NOSE SCAM

Noses

I did a little book—made out of one piece of paper folded over a number of times into a sixteen page mini-book—on noses. Here are a list of nose drawing possibilities, from which I selected fourteen for my book Nosology:

The nose of Kilmajaro.
Nose-feratu.
Palominose.
Monosenucleosis.
Agnosetics.
Diagnoseis.
Cyranose de Bergerac
Onosematapoeia.
Dominose.
Spinosea.
Albinose
Nosetalgia
Enoseis

He has a taste for Blood

115

Performance Artist
and Zen Teacher

I believe that teaching is an art (and, actually, a performance art), and I frequently tell my students, much to their consternation, not to think of me as a professor but, instead, as a "performance" artist. I'm not sure, to be perfectly honest, what a "performance" artist is, I might add, and neither are my students, but this state of mild confusion is very helpful. Students start wondering what is going on and this facilitates involvement. Whatever performance art might be, there is good reason to emphasize the performance aspects of teaching.

An article that appeared in the *San Francisco Chronicle* a number of years ago had some interesting statistics. Let me offer some statistics from the article, which was written by a reporter named Lynn Ludlow. She explains that students in lectures don't necessarily pay attention to what the professor is saying and quotes a paper given to an American Psychological Association meeting which said that if a gun were fired randomly at a lecture and students were asked to write down what they were thinking, you'd find: Around twenty percent of the students, men and women, are pursuing erotic thoughts. Another twenty percent are reminiscing about something. Only twenty percent of the students are paying attention to the lecture. Only twelve percent are actively listening. The other students are daydreaming, worrying, thinking about lunch or about religion.

Ludlow's article contains some more interesting information. Around twenty-one percent of the students said they were happy and around twelve percent said they were sad. The other sixty-six percent were "neutral." More than half of the students described their mood as "worry" or concern" and fewer than twenty percent said "happiness" or "joy." Freudians, of course, would not find it surprising that people might think of sex when a gun goes off, but I will not pursue that line of inquiry any further.

I often read parts of this article to my students, early in the semester, when I explain to them that I do not believe in doing a lot of lecturing, but prefer to have "lecture-discussions" in which

I do some lecturing but also explain things that may confuse people or develop ideas in response to questions students ask. I also point out that there are interesting correlations that can be drawn about the statistics in the article. By a curious coincidence, the twenty-one percent who are happy correlates with the twenty percent of the students who were thinking of sex when the gun went off and the twelve percent who were sad correlates with the twelve percent who are actively following the lecture.

Given these statistics, it doesn't seem to make sense to lecture very much. In a class of fifty students, for example, only ten students would be "paying attention" and only six students would be "actively listening." Even if these figures are wrong and one has twice as many students paying attention and listening, lecturing, per se, doesn't seem to be the most efficient way of teaching students. It makes sense to become a "performance artist" and use whatever theatrical techniques are available to get your students involved and your message across.

I sometimes tell my students that in addition to being a performance artist, I am also a "Zen" teacher. I mention how the Zen masters, in the middle ages, took on the personae of clowns and taught by clowning around. I read them a passage from Conrad Hyers' wonderful book, *Zen and the Comic Spirit* in which Hyers (1974, 142) explains that Zen teachers often acted like clowns and used comic techniques such as incongruity, irrationality, absurdity, self-contradiction, triviality, nonsense and shock to teach. The Zen masters actually dressed like clowns at times and used a great deal of humor in their teaching.

I use a great deal of humor when I teach. I push ideas to absurd conclusions, I joke around (but don't tell jokes as a rule), and often force the students to wonder whether or not they are being "put on." One of my students once asked me to raise my right hand when I was being "serious" so he would know when to take notes. Many of my students find my behavior strange and describe my teaching style as "offbeat" or "weird," though many of them seem to appreciate it.

If you look upon humor as a means of introducing a measure of pleasure into a lecture-discussion, and assume that students desire this "pleasure," there are certain benefits to be derived from using humor at random times during the course of a classroom period. Students will tend to be more alert, since they don't want to miss the gratifications they get from the humor. Humor also reduces the tension and anxiety level of the students–though it may also suggest to them (or to some of them) that what is being discussed isn't serious.

Postmodernism

Postmodernism really caught my attention after a lecture I'd given at Seoul National University a few years ago. My host Hyeon Dew Kang said to me, after my lecture, "we're all crazy about postmodernism here." I remembered that, and when I returned to America I started investigating the subject. A short while later Mitch Allen, an editor, asked me to do a comic book on the subject, since I'm an artist as well as a writer, but I couldn't do it. Instead, I wrote my comic murder mystery *Postmortem for a Postmodernist*.

One thing I realized when I started reading postmodernist thinkers and books about postmodernism was that I, without realizing it, had what might be called a postmodernist sensibility. My book *Media Analysis Techniques* can be seen, I would argue, as essentially postmodernist in nature. What it does is explain the basic principles of four methods of analysis—semiotics, psychoanalytic thought, Marxist thought, and sociological theory—and suggest that there is no one method that is best and that all texts can be analyzed by these four methods and many others as well. In short, there's no "one truth" about texts, and different people, with different beliefs and approaches, see different things in the same work of art.

We are then, in a *Rashomonian* world (I discuss *Rashomon* in the next selection in this book). Is there an absolute truth that can be known about what happened in the clearing in that film or are we only able to say that each person, with a different explanation of what happened, is telling the truth—as he or she sees it. There is no one truth to be known; there are, instead, many truths. And that is one of the central tenets of postmodernism. I was, then, a postmodernist *sans connaisance*. What happened when I read the postmodernists is that I found the philosophical underpinnings of this belief I had.

And my mystery, *Postmortem for a Postmodernist*, reflects this, for everyone in the story says different things about everyone else. The same applies, I might add, to all of my other mysteries. One character says that this woman is a virgin and the next character says she's a nymphomaniac. So life becomes a battle to ascertain the truth when we find ourselves with conflicting descriptions and explanations of everything. And no point of view is held as more correct than others.

When I realized that I was a postmodernist, all kinds of questions I'd had about why I thought about things the way I did and why American culture is the way it is resolved themselves. For example, literary critics with different perspectives on things often disagree about a particular work of literature. Now, postmodernist literary theorists tell us that a work of literature is partly created by its readers, each of whom finds a different meaning in any work.

I had recognized that there are many different ways of analyzing a work of literature or popular culture, which I summarized in the phrase "round up the usual suspects." The suspects are different ways of interpreting anything—based on one's discipline, one's values and beliefs, and many other matters. My suspects are semiotics, psychoanalytic theory, Marxist theory, sociological theory, feminist theory and so on. I dealt with these topics earlier in my discussion of myself as being data-free.

One irony about postmodernism is that there are different schools of postmodernism, which raises the question of what postmodernism actually is.

I deal with this problem in my mystery, and have different kinds of postmodernists define the subject for my detective, Solomon Hunter—and, of course, for my readers.

In addition, I had a postmodernist personality—if that's the correct term. I am an ironist, I play lots of language games (and other kinds of games), I write parodies, I've argued that there isn't that much difference between elite and popular culture, and I hold, it turns out, many of the beliefs and attitudes connected with postmodernism.

In Postmodernism or The Cultural Logic of Late Capitalism, Fredric Jameson writes (1991:2,3) "The postmodernists have, in fact, been fascinated precisely by this whole 'degraded' landscape of schlock and kitsch, of TV series and *Reader's Digest* culture, of advertising and motels, of the late show and grade-B Hollywood films, of so-called paraliterature, with its airport paperback categories of the gothic and the romance, the popular biography, the murder mystery, and the science fiction or fantasy novel: materials they no longer simply 'quote,' as a Joyce or Mahler might have done, but incorporate into their very substance."

That's me! Not only have I been fascinated by these things, I've also written about them and in some cases, such as the murder mystery, written them. Some scholars have argued that the mystery story is a modernist genre, being based on rationality and logic, but it is possible to subvert the mystery genre and write postmodernist mysteries, as Paul Auster's work demonstrates.

What postmodernist mysteries do is give readers a postmodern experience, in contrast to explaining postmodern theory. The same applies to other postmodern literary works such as Italo Calvino's *If on a winter's night a traveler* or Georges Perec's *Life:A User's Manual*. These books strike readers as "strange," for they do all kinds of strange things with the novel, subverting it in strange ways. When I read these books I instinctively recognized that there was something strange about them, —that they were, in funny ways, different from ordinary novels. Might it be because they distill and concretize the postmodernist sensibility?

The question is–how much of my postmodernist sensibility is due to my personality and accidents of my life history and how much of this is due to our so-called "cultural dominant," postmodernism? If it was due to our postmodernist culture, that would mean that most everyone has, more or less, the same outlook on life, and I'm not sure that this is the case. Certainly our teenagers are more postmodernist than their parents and most people over fifty. Is that because the impact of postmodernism has been getting stronger and stronger and is now being reflected in younger people? It got started approximately fifty years ago, so theorists tell us, but maybe it only reached critical mass in the last fifteen or twenty years with the explosive development of our mass media. Perhaps the answer is that we're all postmodernists, but some people are more postmodernist than others. Is it possible, perhaps, that postmodernism doesn't exist and is just a fantasy in the minds of French and other theorists?

Rashomon

Rashomon, I've realized in recent years, had a profound effect on me. But more on that shortly. We start with two stories– *Rashomon* and *In a Grove*, written by Ryunosuke Akutagawa (1892-1927), which, together, are only 15 pages long. *Rashomon*

121

furnished the frame for Kurosawa's film and *In a Grove* furnished the main plot—the conflicting testimony by the main characters of the film about what really happened in the grove.

The Characters in Rashomon. All we can be certain of from the story and the film is that: 1. The bandit, Tajomaru, lured the samurai Takehiro to a grove; 2. Tajomaru overpowered Takehiro and tied him up. 3. Then Tajomaru had sex with Takehiro's wife Masago, who Tajomaru had brought to the grove (saying Takehiro had been bitten by a snake), as Takehiro looked on. 4. Later, Takehiro was found dead.

Whether Tajomaru raped Masago or seduced her is never made clear. We can't be sure. Kurosawa modified Akutogawa's stories slightly for cinematic purposes, but he kept his basic conceit–that people see reality differently, that we are, in a sense, prisoners of our subjectivity. It is useful to think of the basic events in the grove as our primary text or story. That's all we are sure of as "readers" of this text. The main characters, including a woodcutter who happens on the scene, tell their stories, and each gives a very different version, in flashbacks, of what happened.

Tajomaru's Story. Tajomaru suggests, as he recounts his view of what happened, that Masago tried to kill him with a dagger, which only stimulated his desire for her more. She was not raped but willingly had sex with him, however, and his description of the events includes the famous "long kiss" scene in which she is shown closing her eyes and embracing him. That, of course, is his version of the event. After Tajomaru and Masago have sex, he is about to leave when Masago tells him he must fight her husband and she will belong to whomever wins. Tajomaru then says he fought a ferocious battle with Takehiro and they crossed swords more than twenty times before Tajomaru killed him. When he looked around for Masago she was gone.

Masago's Story. In her version, after Tajomaru raped her, he ran off into the forest. She looks at her husband, brokenheartedly, and discovers that he is staring at her, his eyes filled with cruel hatred. Eventually, in something like a trance, to music very much like Ravel's Bolero (which Kurosawa requested) she stabs him with the dagger that she had used to fight off Tajomaru. She then runs away, planning to kill herself, but is unable to do so.

Takehiro's Story. Takehiro's story is told by a medium, who goes into a trance, and enables Takehiro to speak from the grave, through her. As he recounts the tale, after they had sex Tajomaru pleaded with Masago to come with him, and to his surprise, she agrees. But she insists that Tajomaru kill Takehiro. Tajomaru is shocked and repelled by this, throws Masago to the ground, and asks Takehiro what he would like Tajomaru to do to her. Masago runs off, Tajomaru chases after her, but cannot capture her. Hours later he returns, cuts Takehiro's bonds, then goes away. Takehiro, broken hearted, then seizes Masago's dagger and, tears staining his face, stabs himself. As he loses consciousness, he feels the dagger being pulled from his body.

The Woodcutter's Story. This version contradicts all the others. According to the woodcutter, after they have had sex Tajomaru pleads with Masago to marry him and come with him. She says she cannot decide. She says that he must fight Takehiro and cuts the ropes restraining him. To her surprise, and Tajomaru's, Takehiro says he doesn't want to fight for her and that Tajomaru is free to take her. "I cannot risk my life for such a woman," he says, adding that he regrets the loss of his horse more than the loss of his wife. Eventually Masago gets the two men to fight, and their fight is a parody of the samurai story. Both men are terrified and fight in a clownish manner, though at the end Tajomaru does kill Takehiro with his sword (we discover, later, that the woodcutter has stolen the knife and sold it, so he can feed his family, so his version of what happened is not a completely objective one and we cannot trust him any more than we can trust any of the others involved in this film).

The Dilemma. The film poses a dilemma: whom should we believe? And, by implication, can we believe anything or anyone? We have four people each recounting their perspectives on something that happened in a grove and each person tells a credible but completely different story–or, in literary terms, gives a different reading of the events. And since each story is told only from the perspective of the teller, in a flashback, we have no way of knowing who is telling the truth. This is the problem Kurosawa presents us with in *Rashomon*. His film makes us question our view of the world and ourselves and wonder how others might see us–and what they would say if they were called upon, for some reason, to testify about us. *Rashomon* was filmed in 1950 and was made available in a subtitled version in 1952, so we are dealing with a film that is approximately 50 years old.

I think *Rashomon* should be viewed as one of the seminal postmodern texts, for it posed a question to everyone who saw it—what really happened? Who can believed? How do we know who to believe? The notion that there is an absolute truth that everyone can know came under attack; not in a philosophical treatise but in a work of art that had the power to engage the emotions of all who saw it.

When I saw *Rashomon* in 1952, at Smith College, it absolutely bowled me over and, in a sense, now that I think about it, it was the source of my use of multiple perspectives to analyze texts and other topics that catch my attention. *Rashomon* gave me the metaphor that guided me over the last fifty years or so. There is no royal road to analyzing a work of popular culture… or anything. Maybe, especially when it comes to works of art, but also to much of life, we can never know "the truth." All we can know is different people's stories. If I hadn't seen *Rashomon*, I suspect my career as a media critic would have been quite different.

What *Rashomon* did was reflect the postmodern sensibility and make those who saw it have a postmodern experience. I don't think I'd have felt the same way reading a philosophical treatise about postmodernism as I did after I'd seen *Rashomon*, because it worked on my emotions as well as my intellect. It may be that postmodernism has conquered us all (assuming that this is true) because it has been spread by works of art— including music, architecture and other art forms—that have a postmodernist cast to them.

Reviews of My Books:
Making Sense of Mr. Bloom

In the mid-seventies, I published a book (with an introduction by Marshall McLuhan, as I mentioned earlier) which I called *The TV-Guided American*. This book, which offered psychoanalytic and semiotic analyses of some of the most important television programs of the time, was blasted by Jeff Greenfield in *The New York Times*, who concluded his review with the wonderful insult that I offered earlier: *"Berger is to the study of television what Idi Amin is to tourism in Uganda."*

There's nothing like a wonderful line like that, regardless of whether it is positive or negative. Most of the time, reviews don't give you a good line like that—so even the positive ones don't remain in your mind. One person, in review of a manuscript of mine about cultural criticism, said "This book would be a disgrace to Berger, a disgrace to your publishing house, and a disgrace to scholarship."

I was amused by a review of my book *Postmortem for a Postmodernist in Communication Research Trends*. The reviewer wrote,

> "This either is a textbook on postmodernism disguised as
> a mystery novel or a mystery novel disguised as a textbook
> on postmodernism. The fact that you can choose to take
> it as one or the other reflects something of the idea of
> postmodernism that Berger is attempting to put across."

I think the reviewer got it right, and sensed that *Postmortem for a Postmodernist* isn't a textbook, though it has a didactic quality, and isn't a conventional mystery, though it has all the attributes of the mystery novel. It may be its ambiguity that explains why it has been successful, in a modest way.

A Kirkus review of *Bloom's Morning* isn't very positive about my analyses of everyday life in the United States. My book, I should explain, has three parts—the first section is a discussion of sociosemiotics and theory; then there is the middle section, called Ulysses Sociologica, which consists of 35 essays about digital clocks and the like; and finally there is a concluding section that is also theoretical in nature. The heart of the book, as

125

far as I'm concerned, is the middle section "Ulysses Sociologica."

The Kirkus reviewer was not impressed and wrote, "The less convincing centerpiece here—a 'microminimalist' narrative that takes Bloom from wake-up through ablutions to receipt of his mail, followed by 35 explications de texte—reads too often like an overwrought effort to decode what first must be proved to be in code. The digital clock, which 'atomizes' time into discrete, unrelated moments, is an emblem of alienation; the down comforter goes beyond man-made science to 'natural technology.' 'I confess to some tricks—exaggeration, irony, absurdity, wild analogies...whatever it takes,' Berger winks at the end..."

I don't mean to suggest that most of the reviews of my books have been negative. That's not the case at all. One of the nicest reviews I ever got was from a reader who sent me an e-mail message about *Bloom's Morning* that went, in part, "I'm forty-one years old so have grown up postmodern, I suppose, and don't even begin to know the basics. However, from what extremely little I've been able to understand of it, I have been surprised at the resonance I feel with the concept. I think (I think) in postmodern terms which always puts me slightly off kilter with the rest of the world...I took it (*Bloom's Morning*) out of the library, but I'm going to buy it because I want to reread it many times."

She also wrote "I read *Bloom's Morning* this past week—pretty much in one sitting in defiance of my eight-minute attention span. I can't remember the last time I was so thoroughly entertained, enlightened and woken up all at once by a book...I enjoyed each essay, but Breakfast, Garbage Disposals, Bath Soap, and Mail were among my favorites."

There aren't too many writers who can get a fan letter from someone turned on by an analysis of garbage disposals. The readers of *Bloom's Morning*, if this message is typical, were dedicated—but, alas, few in number—and after three months, my publisher remaindered it. It lives on, however–it was translated into German and published there and has also been translated into Chinese...and it is also available at IUniverse.com, a print-on-demand publisher, which has a reprint program.

Roxbury Memorial High School for Boys

I had what could be best described as an bizarre education at Roxbury Memorial High (for Boys), which I discussed earlier. Most of my teachers, if I remember correctly, were Catholic (and many of them Irish Catholics) and from Catholic universities like Holy Cross and Boston College. I went to school between 1947 and 1950, so we're talking about the way schools were more than sixty years ago...though I believe Roxbury Memorial, even in the 1940s, had its feet planted squarely in the Middle Ages.

Roxbury Memorial was an ugly, square monolith that was about ten blocks from where I lived. It was divided into two parts–one for boys and one for girls—and never the two (so the educational authorities hoped) would meet. There was a wall between the two schools, but there was a door in the wall, so some movement back and forth was at least possible. The one redeeming feature of the school was that there was a public library wedged between the schools, on one side–a library where I was to spend a great deal of time.

There were three sequences in the school: a college curriculum, full of Jewish kids (Roxbury was mostly Jewish in those days); a business curriculum; and a trade curriculum, training printers (in the basement of the school). I attended Roxbury Memorial High a long time ago, but I still remember a number of my teachers. There can best described as a congress of zanies, one crazier and more eccentric than the next. It may be that teaching high school students does that to people, though in those days students seemed to be much more motivated and we had fewer distractions. I seem to remember that some of the teachers at Roxbury Memorial (though none of my teachers) might be described as being, in the same way that women can be partially pregnant, mildly anti-Semitic. They must have found it difficult dealing with all those little Jewish kids who were taking the college program, some of whom ended up at Harvard.

Let me start with "Preacher" Kearns. "Preacher" Kearns (I forget his first name) was a dour, very religious man, who was my geometry teacher. He had jet black hair that he plastered down on his head, with a part in the middle. He also had ten children. What was most bizarre was that he had all his students pray before taking exams that they would do well in them. I can remember praying, as hard as I could, that I would do well in my plane geometry quiz.

"Dear God: let me remember that a straight line is the shortest distance between two points," I would pray.

Curiously enough, I carried this habit with me all through high school and even into my first year of college, at the University of Massachusetts. There, one morning, as I was praying before some exam, I suddenly realized what was happening. "What the hell am I doing?" I asked myself. And that was the end of my pre-exam praying. Nowadays, in the age that is interested in meditation and similar things, we might take more kindly to the notion of clearing one's head before undertaking some task, but the prayers I learned from Preacher Kearns were for good grades and God's mercy.

"Dear God. May you have made the professor ask the questions I prepared for," I prayed.

One of my teachers, Andy Gemmel, was called "The G-Man." That was because in the middle of a sentence he would suddenly disappear. He would run out of the room and dash into a bathroom to see whether anyone was smoking. The G-man also worked as a painter during summers and used to talk about how he lugged huge forty-foot ladders around. He was bald, had gray hair and gray eyes, if I remember correctly.

I learned I was an iconoclast from Mr. D. Mr. D always had the smell of menthol cough drops on his breath. This was, we all assumed, to hide the smell of alcohol. D's face was pink and blotched and we all assumed that he was a hard drinker. He said to me once, "Berger, you're an iconoclast." I think I was in the eleventh grade. I went home, looked the word up, and decided it fit. So when I was as young as sixteen, I was already "at war" with conventions and with commonly accepted notions of what makes the world go around. Labeling theory suggests that we often become what we are labeled. God only knows what would have happened to me had Mr. D said "Berger, you're a hidebound conformist."

The "Boss" as he was known, was head of the "Patrol," a group of exemplary students who patrolled the corridors, keeping order and engaged in a war to the death with student smokers.

"Boss" Reardon had confiscated a number of weapons that students had brought to school over the years–baseball bats, pool cues, slingshots, and so on. He taught civics or something like that, because I can remember his tests. He would have us memorize the first paragraph of the Declaration of Independence and his examinations would be as follows: 1. What is the third word after the fourth "and"? 2. What is the fifth word after the second "the"? 3. What is the fourth word after "truths"? He built a platform under his desk that was about eighteen inches high and so he could peer down on his students as they listened to his lectures and wrote their examinations, reciting the Declaration of Independence to themselves and trying to figure out what the fourth word after the third "and" in that text might be.

Then there was Morris Greyser, my art teacher. Since I had studied art in the Saturday program at the Museum of Fine Arts in Boston and was fairly well accomplished as an artist, I was one of his favorites. He liked being an art teacher because he could sneak into his supply room and smoke cigarettes. He was most famous for disciplining students by having them put numbers in pieces of graph paper (they must have been around four or five inches square). He had a huge pile of these slips of graph paper.

If you were talking in class or doing something else, Greyser would say "Do three." If you asked why or questioned his authority, he would add more slips. "Do five, wise guy," he would say. I became, like many others, quite adept at putting numbers from 1 to 99 in the slips of graph paper and then starting all over again until I had filled them out.

Miss McKay was one of the few civilized persons teaching at Roxbury Memorial High School. She was a handsome woman who had a wonderful sense of dignity about her. Her subject was speech. She arranged for students in her speech class to perform on the radio, and every once in a while we would go to some radio station in Boston and act out some story, live on the air, while a musician with an organ supplied music in the background.

It's amazing to think that I went to Roxbury Memorial High more than fifty years ago. Yet the image of a number of my teachers, the crazier ones, still lingers in my mind. I had other teachers whose names I can't remember, but I can recall that one of them had gone to Bates College and thought I would be happy there. I had a government teacher, Dr. Donovan, a beefy man with a pink complexion, who worried about what might happen in Southeast Asia (especially Vietnam), and the usual variety of gym teachers, French teachers, shop teachers and so on. Donovan turned out to be right about Vietnam.

Two or three students from my class went on to Harvard and others went to many other colleges. Of course, like many high schools in Boston, we had a number of students who couldn't "survive" at Boston Latin School and retreated to regular high schools. Many of these students were extremely intelligent but either couldn't or wouldn't do the work that was required at Boston Latin school. My teachers had suggested I go to Latin school but I refused to even consider it. For one thing, I didn't want to have to commute. In addition, I didn't want to kill myself competing with everyone and knock myself out with all that Latin and Greek. Many of the students who left Boston Latin were "burned out" at the tender age of fifteen or sixteen.

I wonder whether we learn because of teachers or in spite of teachers. And I wonder how much one's family, one's social class, the expectations which one "naturally" has, and other things like that affect the way one performs in high school and in college. I was the first one in my family to attend a university. Neither my mother or father had gone beyond high school. My brother Jason went to the art school at the Museum of Fine Arts. Before I even set foot in college, I knew that I'd probably go on for an M.A. degree. My piano teacher, a lovely woman named Mrs. Rosenthal, had said to me during one of our lessons "A BA degree isn't very much nowadays. If you're going to go to college, you should go right through to the Master's degree," which, it turns out, is what I did.

130

San Francisco State University

San Francisco State isn't much to look at. The buildings are undistinguished, to put it mildly. And the campus is small, though that makes it easy to get from building to building. The administration building looks like a fortress and probably could withstand attacks by tanks. The campus could even be a prison. I once suggested we declare it as such, and then lobby to enable professors to get paid as well as prison guards.

On the other hand, it is located in San Francisco, one of the best places to live in the United States, if not the best place. A friend of mine, who once taught at San Francisco State (but escaped) described it as a "cesspool of mediocrity." That may or may not be true, but it brings to mind what another friend once told me. "Even at second-rate universities," she said, "you can lead a good life." It was the San Francisco part of San Francisco State University that was the key to my staying there for my entire academic life as a professor.

In looking over my journals I find myself continually complaining about San Francisco State. On May 4, 1978 I wrote:

And when will I be able to escape from this institution
that I find so repugnant? I'm beginning to suspect
never—a victim of the steady state. Besides, where else is
the living so good?

Later I wrote a two-line verse dealing with my feelings about San Francisco State given the lack of mobility in the academic world:

You've got to be grateful
You've a job you find hateful.

I actually had had other offers but I found the idea of leaving the San Francisco area, and Mill Valley, in particular, very difficult to entertain. As George Gerbner, at the time the dean of the Annenberg School of Communication at the University of Pennsylvania put it to me, "You're living in Marin county, Arthur. Where else is it as good?"

I bought a house in Mill Valley in 1970 (now worth more than twenty times what I paid for it), my wife got a job teaching at a community college within commuting distance, and so it made sense to stay at San Francisco State rather than seeking greener pastures. My wife and I love Mill Valley, and we felt the quality of life aspects of our living where we did was more important than the quality of the institutions where we taught.

The saving factor for me was my department, the Broadcast Communication Arts department (now Broadcast and Electronic Communication Arts) which was very supportive and nurturing. I was, for a dozen years, in a small social science department, which I loathed, but I was able to move to the BCA department and salvage my career. I was lucky to be able to do so, thanks, in part, to Stuart Hyde, who was the chair of the Broadcast Communication Arts Department at the time. I was fortunate enough to move to a department that was much more distinguished than the one I had left (that wouldn't take much) and where the members of the department were much nicer. The department had many good, really decent human beings. That may be why the department was so successful. We had a number of really fine people and a number of them were marvelous teachers and excellent scholars.

One thing I did for my new department was to organize it as an eating society. I created "The BCA Gourmet" and arranged for dinners at all kinds of ethnic restaurants in various parts of the city. We ate in Italian restaurants, Thai restaurants, Vietnamese restaurants, and Chinese restaurants. Generally, we'd have between ten and twenty people at these events.

San Francisco State is a teaching institution (and identifies itself as such) and faculty members do a good deal more teaching than faculty members at many other universities. In theory, we are supposed to teach four courses per semester, and some professors do teach that much—though many find a way to slough off the fourth course. Accordingly, the faculty members are not expected to do very much in the way of publishing or research. There are some, of course, who do, but most of the faculty succeeds (by which I mean gets tenure and gets promoted) at San Francisco State by doing all the grunt work that one finds in complex institutions—that is, serving on department, school and all-university committees...that kind of thing. It also helps if one is active in disciplinary organizations and in one's community.

Getting promoted involves "covering all the bases," as one colleague once put it to me. It is possible to assemble a large dossier to pass in, to get promoted to professor, full of records of one's service to the school, to disciplinary organizations, and to the community at large, and never have published a book, or even an article, in one's academic lifetime. Most of the publishing in various disciplines is done by a relatively small number of scholars, who generally teach at institutions with large graduate programs.

And then there is the all-important subject of teaching. One's teaching ability is determined by student evaluations. The students evaluate their teachers by filling out forms that contain questions such as "does your instructor show command of the subject?" One of my colleagues once confided, "Do you think I'm going to give students what they deserve before I'm promoted to professor...and get lousy evaluations? No way!"

That's the prime reason, I would suggest, for grade inflation. Professors give high grades to get good evaluations and administrators complain about grade inflation, but the student evaluations, which the administrators insist upon, are the reasons for grade inflation. It's a vicious circle.

I think there's something about San Francisco State that destroys most of the good people who go to teach there. There are a number of very fine people there, of course–and some of the people who passed through are extraordinary. For example, Vartan Gregorian taught in the history department before departing for the University of Pennysylvania and later held the presidency of Brown University.

I can't put my finger on it, but there's something about the school that is poisonous. Most of the poison, I'd say, comes from the California State University system and the school's administration. I can recall talking with someone at a Borders in the Bay Area where I was giving a reading from one of my books.

"You teach at State, don't you?" said the woman running the readings program.

"Yes," I said.

"I've heard it's a terrible place!" she said.

San Francisco State is, as one faculty member described it, "small-time academia," and host, therefore, to all the petty intrigues and negative aspects of a small-time institution. It also is a pretty crazy place. It had one president who, it was later discovered, sold Chinese beer on the side, without anyone knowing about it. Another president more or less abandoned the place to run away with his girlfriend. Many of its presidents hoped to use it as a launching pad to move on to presidencies at more distinguished institutions, but so far as I know, none have been able to do so.

In the late sixties I wrote a little ditty that describes the way one succeeds at San Francisco State University:

Good on committees,
For which he was cherished,
He never published,
And he never perished!

In recent years, the California State University system decided on a new program of so-called merit pay, to reward its "most outstanding educators," and this has opened a can of worms. For now faculty members are often on committees that decide whether their colleagues, sometimes colleagues from their departments, deserve merit pay. The faculty senate doesn't want this merit pay system but cannot prevent the president from using it. Unfortunately, the faculty union in the CSU is relatively weak and hasn't been able to block the merit pay system or other decisions that involve the corporatization of the CSU system.

When I went to San Francisco State, it had a reputation as a rather dynamic and progressive institution. That image is long gone. Now, it has a largely demoralized faculty and an increasingly authoritarian administration. On paper, of course, it is a democratic institution, but in reality the administration rules—both from afar (the California State University system, with more than twenty universities, is headquartered in Long Beach) and from the campus administration building-fortress. Now the school has increasingly developed the ambience of a prison, with many members of the faculty counting the years until they can retire. When the school offered a "Golden Handshake" a number of years ago, twice as many professors retired as had been anticipated. They couldn't wait to get out, it seems.

I often wonder about our administrators–they have power, but do they deserve it? What have they done, other than working their way up through the system, to merit their power? You can, of course, ask the same question about a lot of people not in the academic world. What's their "claim to fame?" It's a sad fact that many people with big reputations don't deserve them. We have mediocrities on the Supreme Court and in Congress (some would in the White House, too) and running any number of our institutions. How nobodies become somebodies is a question that has long interested me.

In this respect, I can recall Stanley Milgram, a friend of mine from my Paris days (who also had problems with academics), saying that he was surprised to find so many mediocrities at Harvard and a professor who taught at the University of California at Berkeley complaining about her colleagues as a bunch of second-raters. It may be, of course, that academics are, by their very nature, extremely critical of others.

Saussure

Saussure

I read Saussure in 1973 when I was on sabbatical in London, doing research on English popular culture. Reading Saussure's *Course in General Linguistics* was similar, in impact, to my having seen *Rashomon*. I came away from both with a different perspective on things. Saussure, a Swiss linguist, was one of the founding fathers of semiology, the science of signs. I had spent many years treating various phenomena as signs without ever having articulated the idea. What Saussure did is explain to me what I'd been doing. For semiologists, the universe is full of signs and signs are made of two parts—*signifiers* (sounds and objects) and *signifieds* (concepts, what the sounds and objects mean).

Saussure had written *"A science that studies the life of signs within society* is conceivable...I shall call it *semiology* (from Greek semeîon "sign"). Semiology would show what constitutes signs, what laws govern them." That is one of the charter statements of semiology (the term semiotics has now replaced semiology. It comes from the ideas of the other founding father of sign analysis, C.S. Peirce). Peirce had suggested that the universe is made up entirely of signs; everything is a sign and what semioticians had to do was explain how these signs were to be analyzed.

One other idea of Saussure's that I found compelling was that concepts don't have any meaning in themselves. The meanings of concepts are tied to their relations with other concepts, and the most important relationship is opposition. As Saussure put it, "Concepts are purely differential and defined not by their positive content but negatively by their relations with the other terms of the system." The most important aspect of all this is concepts take their meaning by being "what the others are not." I should point out that this idea has been attacked by many scholars. It is not universally accepted.

We make sense of the world, then, Saussure said, by fitting every concept (and other things as well, let me add) into sets of oppositions that help us determine what concepts, and many other things, mean. "Beautiful" doesn't mean anything unless there is "ugly," and "brave" doesn't mean anything unless there is "cowardly." It is the nature of language, then, that makes our minds work the way they do.

I had always wondered about why I could never think of a concept without thinking of its opposite, and it was Saussure who explained why—it is because that's how language works. I then was able to see people watching a text as being something like very powerful computers that could process concepts and their opposites so quickly that the people didn't realize what was going on. Our minds work so quickly that we set up the oppositions and determine what a given person is not—not a villain, but a hero or heroine—that we don't even think about what we are doing.

And it was my task, I decided, to examine texts of all kinds—comic strips, television shows, hamburgers, gel toothpaste, trash compactors–and determine how they generated meaning and, taking a cue from Freud, what their hidden significance might be. When you see things as signs, and not as simply "things," the world becomes a different place. What seem to be trivial art forms, like comics, now have interesting things to reveal. What seem to be simple objects, like toasters, now become much more complex.

So it was Saussure, along with Freud and Marx, who gave me the tools with which to find meaning everywhere, to tap into the secrets of the commonplace. And it was Barthes and McLuhan, among others, who gave me examples of how semiotics can be used. I am not the only one to have been influenced by Saussure. Although most people in the general public have never heard of his name, he is and deserves to be recognized as one of the most influential thinkers of the twentieth century.

137

Secret Agent

In the early 1970s, George Gerbner, the editor of *The Journal of Communication*, asked me to write an article for his journal on how I analyzed popular culture. I wrote a long essay, perhaps thirty pages long, on my methods, listing what I have called "the familiar suspects"—semiotics, Marxist theory, psychoanalytic theory, and so on. My essay was divided into different sections. Gerbner threw out everything in the article except a section called "The Secret Agent," in which I suggested that I functioned like a secret agent, except I was interested in the "secrets" found in the mass media and popular culture. I did a drawing of myself wearing a slouch hat and a raincoat and holding a revolver. It's one of the best caricatures of myself I've ever done.

He published my article under the title "The Secret Agent." I explained in the article that I wanted to discover the secrets in all the things we tend to think of as mindless and of trivial significance and then not sell my discoveries to foreign countries but publish them and make them known to as many people as I could. Barthes had talked about studying "the which goes without saying," and others had talked about "collective representations." As a secret agent, I took it as my charge to analyze anything I found that shed light upon American culture and society. And it was George Gerbner, who had worked in Intelligence during the Second World War, and might have actually been a secret agent, who recruited me into secret gentry.

That's how I became a Secret Agent. I found it a useful idea to explain to my students what I did, and they, in turn, used to call me "The Secret Agent" when talking about me, but never to my face. I also bought an embosser with my name in the middle and around it the words "writer, artist, secret agent." I often stamp it into letters I send people.

People often say to me, playing along with the idea, "if you were a secret agent, you wouldn't tell everyone, would you?"

"Yes, I would," I reply. "I'd be using reverse psychology. If I tell everyone that I'm a secret agent, nobody will believe me."

One thing about secret agents is that they don't reveal very much about themselves—they hold their cards close to their face. I had written that I acted like a secret agent when I analyzed popular culture or whatever, but maybe the characterization holds for more than just analyzing popular culture. It may be that I tell all about the signs that interest me but don't give anything away about myself.

I should mention that in recent years I've turned myself into another super hero, "Decoder Man," though one might argue that all secret agents are implicitly decoder men and vice versa. "Decoder Man" places more emphasis on my work as a semiotician "decoding" various aspects of American culture and other cultures. I discussed this identity earlier in more detail.

I keep recalling what Huizinga wrote in *The Waning of the Middle Ages*:

> The Middle Ages never forgot that all things would be absurd if their meaning were exhausted in their function and their place in the phenomenal world, if their essence did not reach into a world beyond this. This idea of a deeper significance in ordinary things is familiar to us as well, independently of religious convictions: as an indefinite feelings which may be called up at any moment by the sound of raindrops on the leaves or by the lamplight on a table.

Nothing has meaning in itself; everything is a sign of something else, which may be, in turn, a sign of other things. That's what makes being a Decoder-Man so exciting.

Silberman: The Man on a Quest

On most Saturday mornings, for something like twenty years, I went hiking or walking with Ike Silberman. We generally walked for an hour or so and then we'd get a cup of coffee and figure out how to save the world. Ike, also known as Dr. Isaac Silberman, MD, is a neurologist and psychiatrist who graduated from medical school more than fifty years ago. He is, as a judge once put it (dismissing him from jury duty), a "law unto himself."

He has been working on a project to change the way health is delivered by using telephones and other media. It is a quest and he is a quester, a man with a mission. A sense of mission is, according to some scholars, one of the fundamental attributes of American character. I don't want to say that Ike has an idea fixe, because that is too negative. He points out that something like eighty percent of medical problems can be solved over the phone if a specialist has a good description of the problem—one best provided by someone's general practitioner...and can talk to the person with the medical problem. In theory, his system—if ever implemented–will save billions of dollars.

I can remember when the Clintons were trying to change the medical system. He had a three-page description of his project that he wanted to get into somebody's hands. In recent years he's also written one-page "ads" for his plan, seventeen-page descriptions of it, and I think he also has one that's more than fifty pages long. He's very low key so you never get a sense that he's hustling you or anyone else. It's the process that's important and he's got a lot of patience.

"Don't feel bad," I told him. "Remember it took me twenty years to get my book *An Anatomy of Humor* published."

"Yes," he replied, "But I've been working on this project for a lot more than twenty years." And he has.

There are comic elements to Ike's quest. He's always trying to get his project to the attention of important government figures, like the Secretary of Health and Human Services or business men like Larry Ellison. The problem he faces is that implementing his ideas requires a large investment. I suggested that the situation is analogous to setting up Federal Express. You can't just set it up in one corner of the country and have it work. And the medical system is very slow-moving and scared of rapid change.

"If Bush saw a description of my project," Ike said on one of our walks, "He might go for it. Because it will enable him to save billions of dollars on health care, which would leave him more money for tax cuts."

I talk with him about my adventures with editors, my ideas for new books and what's happening with my published books. We talk about our families, about politics, and God knows what else. In the course of our walking, we often come across sites where houses are being built, and often get into discussions with architects and contractors.

I've learned a lot about medicine, too, from these walks. I once suggested (before Ike semi-retired) that I get a white coat and install myself at his office. New patients would come and talk with me. I would say, after listening to them, "I think this case is best handled by my colleague Dr. Silberman." But he wouldn't teach my courses and so nothing ever happened with that idea. You have to count yourself fortunate to have any good friends and even more fortunate to have a friend who listens to you, and Ike is a wonderful listener. At least I *think* he's listening!

In his latest email, sent to me in September, 2014, he writes that he is preparing a three-page description of his plan for restructuring medicine and hopes to send it to Bill Gates and a few other people like Gates.

Templates

A template is a pattern. In thinking about my mysteries, for example, I have a template I generally use: there is a dinner party or some grouping of professors; there is a murder; then my detective interrogates each of the people at the scene of the crime. Each person offers a different description of what happened and a different assessment of his or her colleagues while at the same time offering information on some subject.

In the same light, there is a template that I use to structure my life now that I'm semi-retired and only teach during the fall semester. 1. I check my e-mail to see if there's anything of interest. Sometimes there is. For example, I was invited to give a paper at a conference in Germany by e-mail. And sometimes I get an e-mail request to write something or an e-mail response from an editor saying a manuscript has been rejected or accepted. 2. Mondays, Wednesdays and Fridays, usually in the morning, I go to the gym and work out. 3. On the way home from the gym I often pick up some groceries. 4. I cook dinner and so I usually set the table for dinner and start cooking around 5:00 PM. 5. Every night, before I got to bed, I set the table for breakfast. 6. I write in my journal at odd moments during the day or night. 7. I write at the computer at various times. On Tuesdays and Thursdays, I often do some writing in the morning. On Mondays, Wednesdays and Fridays, I usually write in the afternoon. I never write more than a couple of hours a day. 8. Saturday mornings I take a walk with my friend Ike Silberman. 9. I read the *San Francisco Chronicle*, *The New York Times*, and *The Marin Independent Journal* at odd moments during the day and evening. 10. I watch television at odd moments, generally speaking. Mostly documentaries and nature shows. 11. I have a snack, cereal and milk or cocoa and toast, around 9:00 or 9:30 PM. 12. I read books that I got from the Mill Valley Library or bought from a bookstore.

That's my template—the general design of my week. Before I retired, my classes and committee work shaped my week and provided the template. For most people, it's one's job that offers a template. But the devil is in the details, and they are the significant part of my life. If you're going to be a writer, you have to spend time writing. That means, you structure your life around your writing, and the best way to do that, as far as I'm concerned, is to adopt (and the process is, for most of us, unconscious) a template. Some people would describe this as being "disciplined."

The UK

In 1973-74, when I went to England on a sabbatical, I did research on English popular culture. I was fortunate enough to spend a few weeks, off and on, in a British advertising agency; I met a number of people at the BBC, watched the telly, collected comics, and wrote an ethnography whose title was *A Year Amongst The UK*. I was taking off on a famous study of a tribe called "the IK". In *A Year Amongst the UK*, I dealt with my travails and culture shock in trying to survive in London. It is amazing how different we are, despite sharing (to a degree) the same language. My adopted metaphor was that I was an anthropologist who had been sent to observe the UK, as if they were a primitive tribe, and try to make sense of their culture.

In 1973, when I wrote "The UK," I commented on everything from paint to Wimpy's hamburgers. Here is a section in which I speculate, with sweeping generalizations, about English culture and character: I had come to England to explore English culture and character. Well, I was getting some valuable insights of a kind not likely to be duplicated by the average American visitor. I had plugged into the economia in the most literal sense of the term—at the household level. This meant I had to struggle with the English electrical system, which means that when you buy hairdryers or irons, you get them without plugs, since there are two different plugs (the round ones and the square ones) here.

This, however, is further complicated by the fact that some companies have changed colors for various wires so that you frequently get plugs with one set of instructions and appliances with another, and you must be careful that you put the correct wires into the correct sockets. The plugs frequently come with small fuses, which means that is there is a malfunction or overload, the plug blows and not the system itself.

One day my wife had rushed out to Woolworths to get a hairdryer and came rushing home so she could shampoo her hair and set it in time for a tea to which she had been invited that afternoon.

"At least I got this without the usual fuss and inconvenience," she said, as she plunked down the carton in which the hairdryer came. As she did, a monstrous thought crossed my mind, and

144

what I feared was soon to come true. She opened the box and pulled out the hairdryer. The wire attached to the hairdryer was coiled neatly, and at the end of this wire were three shiny pieces of wire and no plug.

Shorlock Holms

"Damn it," she cried, and I could understand how she felt, for in England we had felt a subtle and diffuse kind of resistance permeating the atmosphere. Somehow, everything we tried to do was absurdly difficult. There was an element of culture shock about this. We were in an unfamiliar ambiance, though we spoke the same language and had many common traditions.

In England we had to grope, somehow, to do even the simplest things. If you didn't mind devoting your life to surviving—going shopping every day, washing clothes every day, doing everything in bits and pieces without much concern for finalities, England posed few problems. You merely waited and did without, until, somehow, you found what you wanted or somebody eventually did what you wanted them to do—install a telephone, turn on the gas, and so on.

I met people in England who spent ten years contemplating certain things they thought they might like to do. I could understand this for the subtle pressure of English culture, which puts people in their place, which contains many privileges for some (at the expense of others), exudes a subtle kind of resistance to change. Everything requires so much effort that after a while you give in.

We had started our year in England with a visit to Battle Abbey and in some curious way that visit had given me a perspective on contemporary English culture. The styles have changed now. Instead of walking about in medieval garb or coats of armor, the modern Englishman wears a suit (and some younger Englishmen wear flared and cuffed elephant pants and high-heeled platform shoes, but the impact of the medieval world is still powerful.

For society now, as then, is divided into two realms—the peasants and the lords (metaphorically speaking) and that division has been and still is all-important. There is in England a large middle class, but the important division is between the worldview and activities of the lords and the peasants, the aristocrats and their servants, the kings and the commoners. Politically this division may not be too important, but psychologically and culturally it remains powerful.

America, Emerson said, is a "land without history." England is a land with too much history. England is a land of the medieval, the father, the past, where everyone has a strong sense of place and of class, where the architecture is that of power. England is a land where ascription is very strong and where aggression is turned inward, so there is a pervasive sense of guilt. America is postmodern, a land of the son, the young, the future, where people are placeless and rootless, where achievement counts and where aggression is turned outward, which helps explain all the violence one finds in the United States.

When I returned home to California, I sent my manuscript to Walker & Co., which had published my book *The Comic-Stripped American*. My editor there didn't think my manuscript was commercial enough, but liked the analyses I had made of some popular British television shows and suggested I write a book on American television shows and use the material on the British shows at the end. I did this and wrote *The TV-Guided American*. Marshall McLuhan was kind enough to write an introduction for the book. It was reviewed by someone in *The New York Times* who didn't like my semiotic and psychoanalytic interpretation of the shows I analyzed. His review concluded with a wonderful insult, "Berger is to the study of television what Idi Amin is to tourism in Uganda."

A woman who lived next door to us in London was a retired typist, who agreed to type my manuscript. When she finished typing it, she turned very hostile, since she didn't like what I said about the English. But she still gave candy to my children. That's one of the things you do when you're a member of the UK.

146

Vietnam of My Imagination

I've read a number of books and articles by travelers in Vietnam. I recall how Pico Iyer's description of Vietnam in his book *Falling Off the Map: Some Lonely Places of the World* struck me and made me curious about the country. His descriptions of the legions of Vietnamese on motorbikes brought back memories of Thailand; in Bangkok and Chang Mai, and most of the other cities I've visited, motorbikes, motorcycles, tuk-tuks, and motorized vehicles of all kinds had an overwhelming presence. They were like army ants on a rampage. You had to watch out for them, for every step was dangerous.

I've also purchased and read a number of tourist guidebooks to Vietnam—the Lonely Planet one, the Rough Guide one, and several others. And in bookstores I've looked at other books about Vietnam, many with photographs. So Vietnam is a collection of images in my mind's eye, as well as a hodgepodge of descriptions of cities, hotels and restaurants and maps, which locate various restaurants and hotels.

So Vietnam will not be, and cannot be, what I (or anyone else) imagines it will be like. The map, it has been said, is not the territory. All that I can hope is that my preparations for my trip to Vietnam will, somehow, lessen the culture shock. On the other hand, it is precisely the matter of culture shock that interests me and is one of the reasons for my trip to Vietnam. I am going to write an ethnography—that is, I will use my personal experiences in Vietnam to draw inferences about Vietnamese character and culture.

One of my models for this enterprise is Roland Barthes' *Empire of Signs*, his study of Japanese culture. In this book he writes: (1982:3) "If I want to imagine a fictive nation, I can give it an invented name, treat it declaratively as a novelistic object, create a new Garabagne, so as to compromise no real country by my fantasy (though it is then that fantasy itself I compromise by the signs of literature). I can also—though in no way claiming to represent or to analyze reality (these being the major gestures of Western discourse)—isolate somewhere in the world (faraway) a certain number of features (a term employed in linguistics), and out of these features deliberately form a system. It is this system which I shall call: Japan."

What Barthes did in *Empire of Signs* is to analyze certain Japanese objects and practices that struck him as significant. His book, then, is an interesting combination of social semiotics and ethnography, or maybe ethno-semiotics, if there is such a discipline, would be a better term. His book has short chapters on Japanese chopsticks, sukiyaki, tempura, pachinko, packages, train stations, stationery stores, spatial organization, and so on.

The important thing is to find signs—objects, practices, phenomena of various kinds—that offer insights into Vietnamese character and culture, in the same way that an individual's facial expressions, body language, voice, dress, and other "tells" offer insights into his or her behavior, personality and character. My travels through Vietnam, then, are to serve as a kind of structure that I hope will enable me to find important signs–revealing topics that I can explore to gain insights into Vietnamese culture. I will be trying, so to speak, if not to read the universe in a grain of sand, to read something about a culture in a bowl of Pho.

I must confess to a certain amount of anxiety about getting diarrhea in Vietnam. Everyone does, so our guidebooks say, but generally it is very mild and you get over it quickly. Still, having suffered from diarrhea a number of different times during our vacations, I can't escape a sense of anxiety. On the other hand, last year in Morocco I was fine. So there is an element of luck in travel and I hope I'll be lucky this time. If not, I have lots of preparations to take care of matters, from over-the-counter remedies to prescription drugs. I love Vietnamese food. We have a Vietnamese restaurant in San Francisco, Tu Lam, its claim to fame being that it was visited by Julia Child. It is a dive—little more than a hole in the wall, but the food is extremely tasty. So I find myself full of anticipation, with touches of anxiety, about our trip to Vietnam. A friend who went there in January said "It's beyond fabulous." I want to find out for myself.

Wildavsky

I met Aaron Wildavsky at a party in Berkeley in 1972. I had been granted a sabbatical to spend a year in England, studying English popular culture, and a friend told me about a party where I could meet someone who had just come back from England. I had called the host and hostess to ask whether it would be okay for us to come and were told they would be delighted to have us there. But we didn't know anyone there and so we found ourselves lingering on the sidelines, so to speak, with someone else—a bald, bearded fellow, with whom we struck up a conversation. He told me his name was Aaron Wildavsky, and that he taught at the University of California. His name, at the time, meant nothing to me. An analogous situation would be meeting someone at a party who told you his name was Ted Williams and not knowing who he was. I am not a political scientist so I didn't realize I was chatting with the man who was, perhaps, the most important political scientist of his time.

We started telling jokes—he told some wonderful Jewish jokes– and chatting about this and that and decided to swap articles about popular culture that we had written. I liked his sense of humor and suggested that we get together some time, when we returned from England. He agreed, so we took down each other's name and address and that was that.

And so, in 1973, we rented out our house and moved to London for a year, where I rented an old house in Golders Green that was owned by a friend of a friend of mine. One morning, I was walking down a street in the middle of London when who should I bump into but Aaron Wildavsky. It turned out that his former wife and their children were living in London, and he game me their address and phone number so we could get together. I called and we arranged to celebrate Thanksgiving with them...and we saw them at other times as well.

When we returned to America, I called Aaron and we arranged to see one another. He married a woman he met in England and

149

bought a beautiful house in the Oakland hills. Over the years, we saw Aaron and Mary Wildavsky a number of times. Aaron had the face I could caricature very easily, and I drew a number of caricatures of him. My favorite was one in which he is speaking to a king, sitting on a throne. The king looks exactly like him. He is saying to the king, "You're wonderful." The caption for the cartoon was "Speaking Truth to Power," the title of one of his books.

In the early eighties I had written a manuscript for a book on four different ways of analyzing films, television programs, advertisements—what academics call "texts." I had written a chapter on semiotic analysis for someone doing a book on methods of analysis, for which I was supposed to get the princely sum of $150. I never got it. So, having a chapter on the basic principles of semiotics, I thought it might make good sense to write three more chapters, on Marxist, Freudian or psychoanalytic, and sociological principles, to form the "theory" part of a book on criticism. In the second part of the book, on applied criticism, I had chapters on the four ways of interpreting blue jeans.

I sent the manuscript to the communications editor at Sage publications and it was rejected. Shortly after, I was over Aaron's house and mentioned to him that I had a manuscript that I thought would be very useful, but it had been rejected.

"Why don't you send it to me," he said. "I know someone who might be interested."

So I sent it to him and he sent it to Sage publications, to the sociology editor, Mitch Allen, and it was accepted. But it was decided that since the book would be most useful for media studies courses, I should write four new chapters for the applications section of the book. I agreed, and then I thought about what I deal with. I concluded that I would take topics that had lasting power, and so I took advertising, all-news radio, football, and a fine detective film, *Murder on the Orient Express*. I showed how various aspects of the four theories could be used to analyze my four topics. My revision was accepted and Sage published the book.

Its reception exceeded our fondest hopes and it turned out to be my bestselling book. It has been reprinted something like twenty-five or thirty times, and now is in its second edition. In this edition I replaced my chapter on advertising with a new chapter I wrote, analyzing one particular advertisement—the famous "girl with the snake" advertisement for Dior perfume.

I believe it was Aaron who put me in touch with Irving Louis Horowitz at *Transaction*. Curiously, Horowitz had published my first article to be published in America in Transaction magazine (now *Society*). The lead article in that issue was, by chance, by Aaron Wildavsky.

Aaron and I talked about collaborating on a book of humor, but before we could do very much, he passed away. I can remember talking with him shortly before he found out that he had lung cancer. He had gone to the doctor complaining about a pain in his shoulder. The doctor gave him an injection, but it didn't do any good. So Aaron went back again and the doctor ordered a chest x-ray.

"It doesn't look very good," he said to me, and then he told me what the doctors had found. Lung cancer, and a very pernicious kind. The doctors had told him he had three months to three years to live. He thought he'd have the three years but it was only three months. By the time he died, at 63, he had published an incredible number of seminal articles and more than thirty major books.

I remember him as an extraordinarily kind man. Once, when we were walking in a park in Oakland, he mentioned a book he had read by a professor in a small and not particularly influential college.

"You know," he said, "You don't have to be in a major research institution to make important contributions to scholarship."

I got his message.

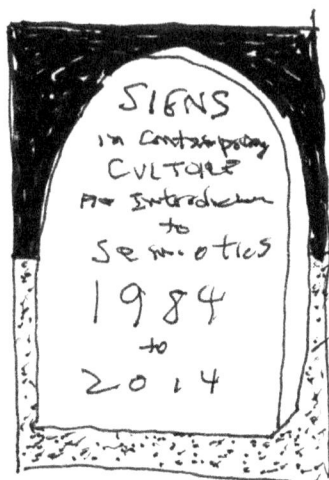

Writing Myself Into Existence

I am a study in self-creation. I almost feel that I've written myself into existence in my journals. I developed my mind, my style, and my sense of myself—with liberal borrowings from here and there. I may be a fictional character or imaginary being who believes himself real? Who knows?

That's what I wrote on the first page of my 32nd journal, *Relations*, on March 7, 1976. Now, more than twenty-five years later, I see myself as a writer who happened to teach, in contrast to being a teacher who happened to write. I also believe that my writing helped me be a better teacher, since I often had new ideas and new material to share with my students.

I've spent something like forty years in university classrooms with students. Almost universally, my students have said that they'd never had anyone like me before for an instructor (with the implication, in some cases, that one experience was enough)—though I never could see what was so idiosyncratic or unusual about the way I ran my courses.

My first book was my Ph.D. dissertation on *Li'l Abner*. I decided to send it to Twayne publishers, on the advice of a friend. Then I didn't hear from them for a year plus. I happened, by chance, to be in New York and went to see the editor of Twayne books.

"Berger," he said, as I sat down on a chair in front of his desk. "What are we going to do about your book? I don't remember."

He reached behind him and pulled my manuscript from a bookcase. He opened the book.

"We're going to publish it," he said.

I can remember how thrilled I was. I thought, at that time, that publishing a book would make a big different in my academic career, and also how little trauma it took to get a book published. Maybe that success encouraged me to continue writing, because after five or six years I found myself with six books. I never thought I'd write many more books, but somehow I got ideas for different books and before too many years had passed, I had twelve books. Then, not too much later, somehow I had twenty-four books, and then forty books. I can't explain it. From my list of books you can get a sense of my interests. One reason my books were published was because they were "accessible." That means I didn't thrown fancy jargon around or write in the style that many graduate students learn, which is highly stylized and often quite pretentious.

Publishing books is often quite aggravating, for a variety of reasons. Copy-editors go over your manuscripts and ask millions of questions. When you've gone over the page proofs and taken care of the index, you find that there are frequently long delays at the printers. Sometimes your editors make all kinds of suggestions, and they often send your manuscripts to professors who make other suggestions and at times really want you to rewrite the book the way they would have written it. Or who trash the book. Here's a jointly written review of my *Mass Comm Murders* manuscript that shows what I'm talking about. I don't know the names of the authors of this review:

> *As written we are hard pressed to think of any courses for which this book would be value added. It would confuse rather than clarify. In contrast, we think that the edited book that Haddley-Lassiter [a character in my mystery who strings together quoted passages from famous theorists in a proposal for a book] would be a good companion volume to any Mass Communication Theory text...we cannot think of a media and/or theory text that would be enhanced by being used with Murder Go Round [the original title for my book]."*

The review then concluded that I should rewrite the book along lines the authors suggest and come up with a completely different book:

> *Such a rewrite would require Berger to start over. As it is now, the narrative in no way elucidates theory—it's*

P ROGRESS
REPORT

Tuesday, July 17, 2012
LOTS to report..
TRAVEL
1. Argentina.. I'm going there for a month, from April 24th until
September 24th. To lecture, etc.

2. South India ... we are planning the visit South India from Jan. 18–
Feb 6th.. with a two day stay in Dubai. To get over the 15 hour
flight from SF to Dubai.

BOOKS
1. Theorizing Tourism ... I revised it and Mitch Allen is looking
it over. More rewriting may be needed ... or demanded !!

2. Media, Myth & Culture.. Polgrave/Macmillan. I have a
contract but nothing seems to be happening

3. Media + Communication Research Methods.. Being revised.
Due Jan. 15, 2013.

4. Media Analysis Techniques Being revised. Due June 15,
2013.

    We're repairing the deck.. doing part of it.. it should be done
in a couple of days ... The lumber cost $135 and I probably have
to get another $100 worth of lumber ... I'm paying the carpenter
$30 an hour.

    Phyllis is on the Marin Grand Jury.. That's a year long com-
mitment.. I believe she'll go in two days a week... Gabriel now
works for Google... + Juno has a job as well.. part time. He'd like
to work for himself ... but I don't see him doing that for the near
future...

Wed. July 18, 2012 (cloudy) → SUN
    I fell asleep at 11:30 PM & got up at 4:00 AM.. I rested
in bed until 7:00 AM. Aille Hyde died.. She was about 86, we
assume.. There was a strike in the IJ. I had breakfast at 7:00 &
my stomach is bothering me a bit.. I wonder whether it's from
the Chivos marmalade?
    Now I'm waiting to see when Bobby comes. He came at
11:45 -- with another person. He plans to finish today. I hope so...

simply a fairly clever story with fragments of theory thrown in rather haphazardly.

Reading a manuscript review like this helps explain, I think, why bumping off professors can be therapeutic (the book was published and is doing quite well, incidentally). And this review is not the most negative review I've ever received. Someone reviewed one of my books, in a Canadian journal, by writing "How do you review a book that never should have been written?" I should point out that sometimes you get valuable suggestions from the reviewers to whom your editors send your manuscripts.

I like to illustrate my own books, so I've been fortunate to find some publishers who have made excellent use of my illustrations. There is a momentary thrill you get when your publisher finally sends you a copy of your new book. This is followed by speculations about how the book might be reviewed and doubts about whether anyone will read it or any professors will adopt it for their classes. When I get a new book I look the book over, scan it for typos, and then I put it in my book case. Then, it's on to the next book. That's because by the time one of my books is published, I've spent so much time working on it—going over the manuscript many times to get the writing just right, going over the copy edited manuscript pages, proofreading the page proofs, making the index—that I'm sick and tired of the book... but very happy that it has been published.

It's always interesting for me to watch people in bookstores. They pick up a book, glance at the front and back cover, look at the table of contents, and put it down, all in about a minute's time. When I think of the amount of work involved in writing the book and publishing it, I always marvel that books are treated in such a cavalier manner. But, of course, I'm speaking from the perspective of a writer.

There is something else I should mention. Unlike many authors who write textbooks (I don't think of myself as writing textbooks but as writing scholarly books that are used as textbooks), I never write queries to publishers about books I plan on writing. Instead, I write the book—because I'm interested in the subject, because I want to find out more about it, and because I want to discover what ideas I had that I never recognized until I started writing. And then I go looking for a publisher.

So every book of mine represents a lot of work that may not pay off in getting published. Now that I have a substantial number of books that have been published, writing a book before getting a commitment from a publisher isn't quite as risky as it used to be. But it still is a risk and I must confess that I'm not always successful in publishing books I've written.

And books don't always have the "payoff" you think they'll have. In my 35th journal, Relations II, I write:

> So here I am with my seventh and eighth book coming out andit has meant nothing, so it seems. No job offers, no help in getting grants, no help at school (in fact, it has hindered me). It has given me a lot of psychic income and ego strength, however…and some regular income, as well.

One problem with writing oneself into existence is that you face a problem when you stop writing. Will you cease to exist? That may suggest that when I complain to myself, in my journals, as I do over and over again, that I haven't got any ideas for new books, I'm really alluding to an existential dilemma that I, and all writers, unconsciously recognize. Maybe we can modify Berkeley and say that for writers, "To be is to be in print" or "To be is to be reviewed," or some combination of the two. In any case, there's hardly been a day in my life that I didn't write something in my journal or in an article or a book I'm working on. My latest book is called *Messages: An Introduction to Communication.* I did the pastiche/collage used on the cover.

Messages:An Introduction to Communication

Zadkine

In 1958 I went to visit Ossip Zadkine, the famous sculptor, at 2:00 PM one afternoon, intending to stay for half an hour, and ended up staying five hours. My brother Jason had studied with him, many years before. It was an utterly amazing experience. Zadkine's a short, slender man who, at seventy, is still very active. A journalist from *France-Soir* spent an hour or so talking with him, taking notes on his remembrances of Modigliani, Radriguet and other giants of French arts and letters. The journalist left and a group of Zadkine's friends came, and then he started a series of stories that were incredibly beautiful and mesmerizing. We were all hypnotized as Zadkine told us stories about his experiences with rats.

Adventure one: One day he discovered a rat in his studio and was fascinated by the shape of its head. He stood watching the rat for a long time, then the rat ran and hid somewhere in Zadkine's studio. Zadkine hunted for every opening and barricaded any opening that he found. The rat tunneled under these barricades and came up in the kitchen and one day it ran off with a lamb chop that Zadkine was going to cook. Zadkine had other adventures with the rat but finally decided to do away with it, so he got a piece of cake, soaked it in poison, and left it for the rat. The rat couldn't resist. It ate the cake, ran away, and never was seen again.

Adventure two: One day Zadkine found a pigeon that had been hurt…it had hurt its wing. So Zadkine gave it something to eat. A group of rats that had gathered along the Seine were wandering around and smelled the pigeon. They tunneled under the wall that surrounds Zadkine's garden and ate the pigeon. Zadkine came upon them as they were eating the pigeon and they ran into his studio. He ran and grabbed a big stick and waited for them to come out of his studio…he waited many hours, but they didn't reappear.

Adventure three: An American pianist had a studio near the mansion of the Princess Bibesco, in a cellar apartment. He moved in and started playing. As he struck the first chord he hear a scratching sound and jerked his head around to see what it was. He continued playing and the scratching continued, as the rats gathered near to hear the concert and he continually turned his neck to see what was causing the scratching. After several weeks he gave up playing the piano and spent his time listening to the rats scratching. He became very irritable, found he couldn't stop twitching his head, and forgot about the music. Eventually he packed up and left the apartment.

I think he decided to talk about his adventure with rats because there was an article in *Le Monde* written by some French doctors who had toured China and written that there were no longer any rats in China.

Zadkine said that sculptors are very similar to cabinet makers. They make chairs that are so comfortable that when you sit in them you say "I've never been in a chair quite like this before." And there are various kinds of chairs...some are so simple you can make two chairs a day, but others you work and work on... and they just never seem to get to be finished. He said that he doesn't travel much because he doesn't have the time. He's never been in an airplane. "It's like getting married," he said of flying.

I told him that I had just got out of the Army and now I was drifting a bit. "It's worth taking a year off and drifting, if you keep your eyes open," he replied.

Zadkine's stories about his adventures with rats brings to mind a wonderful joke:

> Three rabbis are discussing their problems with mice in their synagogues. The first rabbi said "When I discovered I had mice, I called an exterminator. He came and gassed the mice and most of them died. A few days later the mice came back and I don't know what to do." The second rabbi said, "when I discovered we had mice in our shul I bought some cats, but they couldn't keep up with the mice. I don't know how I'm going to get rid of them." "You should do what I did," said the third rabbi. "When I discovered I had mice in the shul, I gathered them all together into a group and Bar Mitzvahed them. I've not seen one since!"

And that is how I will leave you, with a Jewish joke.

Sole
Arthur
Alimentary my Dear Watson
EXTRA ECCLESIA NULLA SALUS
Porque?
ARTHUR ASA BERGER
0-582-28487-2

Coda

On September 1, 2015, I wrote in my journal (Number 96, titled "*Iran Apotheosis*," page 84, "I've still not figured out what my next project will be. Maybe I've written myself out." This is, considering what I'm involve with at the moment, rather strange. I have this book, *Writing Myself Into Existence,* being published, I have the fourth edition of my book *Media and Communication Research Methods* about to be published, I have a new book on digital devices and culture, *Gizmos,* at a copyeditor in India, a new book tentatively titled *Applied Discourse Analysis,* at a publisher who has tentatively accepted it but wants revisions, and a collection of articles on media, pop culture and related concerns, tentatively titled *Critical Modalities,* being considered for publication. It isn't unusual for me to have a number of books being published and others being considered for publication at the same time. One year, if I recall correctly, I published five books.

But I am now, as my wife Phyllis (who has been married to me for 54 years) put it, "at loose ends." That's because I don't have an idea for a new book project in mind, and when that's the case, I tend to become restless and start wondering whether I have written my last book. I often have this feeling. I'm starting to play around with ideas in my journal and, no doubt, sooner or later I'll have an idea. I haven't written an academic murder mystery in a while and I might write one while I figure out what other books I might want to do. Fortunately, I have my journals. If you spend fifteen or twenty minutes a day on a journal, after fifty years you end up with 96 journals, plus a dozen other travel journals I kept in separate notebooks. I might want to use them to do another book on travel.

If writing yourself into existence is the way you convince yourself that you are still alive, when you aren't writing it's not writers block. It's an existential crisis.

Arthur Asa Berger

Bibliography

Books by the Author

Ads, Fads & Consumer Culture, 2000. (Rowman & Littlefield)

Agitpop: Political Culture and Communication Theory, 1989 (Transaction)

An Anatomy of Humor, 1993. (Transaction)

Art of Comedy Writing, 1997 (Transaction)

Bali Tourism. 2013. (Haworth).

Blind Men & Elephants: Perspectives on Humor, 1995 (Transaction)

Bloom's Morning, 1997 (Westview/HarperCollins) (German edition, 1998) (Chinese edition, 2001)

Comic Stripped American, 1974 (Walker & Co., Penguin, Milano Libri)

Cultural Criticism: A Primer of Key Concepts, 1995 (SAGE) (Swedish edition, 1998)

Cultural Theorist's Book of Quotations. 2010. (Left Coast Press)

Durkheim is Dead: Sherlock Holmes is Introduced to Social Theory, 2003 (AltaMira Press)

Essentials of Mass Communication Theory, 1995 (SAGE)

Evangelical Hamburger, 1970 (MSS Publications)

Genius of the Jewish Joke, 1997 (Jason Aronson)

Gizmos: How Digital Devices Have Transformed American Character and Culture. (Pivot)

Jewish Jesters, 2001. (Hampton Press)

Kabbalah Killings. 2004. (PulpLit)

Li'l Abner, 1970 (Twayne), 1994 (Univ. of Mississippi Press)

Mass Comm Murders: Five Media Theorists Self-Destruct. 2002 (Rowman & Littlefield).

Media & Communication Research Methods, 2000. (SAGE)

Media Analysis Techniques, 1982, 2nd Edition 1998 (SAGE). 5th Edition. 2014.

Messages: An Introduction to Communication. 2014 (Left Coast Press)

Mistake in Identity:A Cultural Studies Murder Mystery 2005. (AltaMira)

Narratives in Popular Culture, Media & Everyday Life, 1997 (SAGE) Chinese edition (2000)

Pop Culture, 1973 (Pflaum)

Postmortem for a Postmodernist, 1997 (AltaMira).

Seeing is Believing:An Introduction to Visual Communication, 1989, 3rd edition 2008 (McGraw-Hill).

Shop Till You Drop:Perspectives on American Consumer Culture. 2004. (Rowman & Littlefield)

Signs in Contemporary Culture, 1984 (Longman); 2nd edition, Sheffield, 1998. (Indonesian edition, 2003)

Television as an Instrument of Terror, 1978 (Transaction)

Television in SOCIETY, 1986 (Transaction)

Thailand Tourism. 2008. (Haworth Hospitality and Tourism Press)

The Golden Triangle. 2008. (Transaction Books).

The Objects of Affection: Semiotics and Consumer Culture. 2010. (Palgrave)

Theorizing Tourism. 2012. (Left Coast Press).

Tourism in Japan:An Ethno-Semiotic Analysis. 2010 (Channel View Publications)

TVGuided American, 1975 (Walker & Co.)

Understanding American Icons:An Introduction to Semiotics. 2012. (Left Coast Press).

Vietnam Tourism. 2005. (Haworth)

What Objects Mean:An Introduction to Material Culture 2009. (Left Coast Press)

Year Amongst the UK: Notes on Character and Culture in England 1973-1974. Marin Arts Press.

Other Books and Publications

Barthes, Roland. (1972). *Mythologies.* New York: Hill & Wang

Barthes, Roland. (1982). *Empire of Signs.* New York: Hill & Wang

Calvino, Italo. (1982) *If on a winter's night.* New York: Harcourt Brace Jovanovich

Christie, Agatha. (1940) *Murder on the Orient Express*.
New York: Pocket Books.

Communication Research Trends

Epoca

Europeo

Huizinga, Johannes. (1954). *The Waning of the Middle Ages*.
New York: Anchor.

Iyer, Pico. (1993). *Falling Off the Map: Some Lonely Places of
the World*. New York: Vintage.

Journal of Communication

Le Monde

Los Angeles Times

Marin Independent Journal

Minnesota Daily

McLuhan, Marshall. (1967). *The Mechanical Bride: Folklore of
Industrial Man*. Boston: Beacon Press.

The New York Times.

Oggi

Perec, Georges. (1987) *Life: A User's Manual*.
New York: Godine.

San Francisco Chronicle.

Saussure, Ferdinand de. (1966). *A Course in General
Linguistics*. New York: McGraw-Hill.

Theall, Donald. (2006). *The Virtual Marshall Mcluhan*.
Montreal: McGill-Queens University Press.

Transaction

The Washington Post.

Young, Marguerite. (1965) *Miss Macintosh My Darling*.
New York: Scribner's.

About The Author

Arthur Asa Berger is the author of more than one hundred articles and more than seventy books on pop culture, media, cultural studies, humor and tourism. If you count second, third, fourth and fifth editions of books, he has published more than ninety books. His books have been translated into ten languages, with fourteen of his books translated into Chinese and five into Farsi. One of his favorite articles was titled "*The Evangelical Hamburger.*" It was a study of McDonald's hamburgers and American culture, published in 1964. He also wrote an article published in the *Los Angeles Times* about some sexual aspects of video games. His book *Bloom's Morning* psychoanalyzed kitchen appliances and other household objects and rituals and includes drawings he made for each chapter. When he gave a reading on the book in Vietnam, someone in the audience asked him if the book was a work of fiction. That is the way many serious scholars in the United States look upon all his writings.

He delights in taking obscure theories generally written in impenetrable prose by European scholars and pushing them to absurd results. He has explained the way he writes as follows—"I make everything up as I go along and throw in charts and diagrams to fool social scientists." Jean Baudrillard writes in his *Fragments*, "He who speaks of himself should never say the whole truth, he should keep it secret and divulge only fragments." Berger has taken this advice to heart.

NeoPoiesis: *a new way of making*

1) in ancient Greece, poiesis referred to the process of making: creation - production - organization - formation - causation

2) a process that can be physical and spiritual, biological and intellectual, artistic and technological, material and teleological, efficient and formal

3) a means of modifying the environment and a method of organizing the self, the making of art and music and poetry, the fashioning of memory and history and philosophy, the construction of perception and expression and reality

4) an independent publisher with a steadfast goal to print and promote outstanding poets, writers and artists that reflect the creative drive and spirit of the new electronic landscape

NeoPoiesisPress.com

www.ingramcontent.com/pod-product-compliance
Lightning Source LLC
Chambersburg PA
CBHW071343090426
42738CB00012B/2995